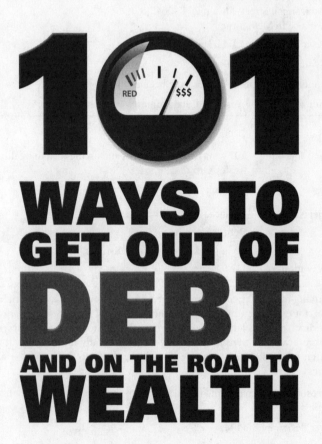

101
WAYS TO
GET OUT OF
DEBT
AND ON THE ROAD TO
WEALTH

Ashley Ormond

Wrightbooks

First published 2009 by Wrightbooks
an imprint of John Wiley & Sons Australia, Ltd
42 McDougall Street, Milton Qld 4064
Office also in Melbourne

Typeset in Berkeley LT 11/14pt

© Ashley Ormond 2009

The moral rights of the author have been asserted

National Library of Australia Cataloguing-in-Publication entry:

Author:	Ormond, Ashley.
Title:	101 ways to get out of debt and on the road to wealth/ Ashley Ormond.
ISBN:	9781742169361 (pbk.)
Subjects:	Finance, Personal—Australia.
	Debt—Australia.
	Saving and investment—Australia.
Dewey number:	332.02401

Microsoft Excel screenshots reprinted with permission from Microsoft Corporation

Cover design by Brad Maxwell

Cover image © Alhovik, 2009, used under license from Shutterstock.com

Printed in Australia by McPherson's Printing Group

10 9 8 7 6 5 4 3 2 1

Disclaimer
The material in this publication is of the nature of general comment only, and does not represent professional advice. It is not intended to provide specific guidance for particular circumstances and it should not be relied on as the basis for any decision to take action or not take action on any matter which it covers. Readers should obtain professional advice where appropriate, before making any such decision. To the maximum extent permitted by law, the author and publisher disclaim all responsibility and liability to any person, arising directly or indirectly from any person taking or not taking action based upon the information in this publication.

Personal debt is the devil for people trying to build wealth. In this very practical book Ashley Ormond shows us many ways to beat the devil and get on the road to riches.

—Pam Walkley
Editor-in-chief, *Money* magazine

Debt can be a great servant, but a bad master. In this book Ashley will show you simple ways to take control of your debts, and make debt a tool you can use and not something to fear.

—Noel Whittaker
Best-selling author and finance columnist, *The Sydney Morning Herald* and *The Age*

Australians have been living beyond their means on a diet of cheap debt for too long. This is a must-read book for all those who want to get out of debt and back in control of their finances.

—Chris Cuffe
Former CEO, Colonial First State

Many Australians live beyond their means and take on too much debt. Ashley Ormond's book is by far the best account yet available on understanding the details of debt, the problems that arise when debt becomes excessive and how we can manage and reduce debt to achieve better financial security and happiness for ourselves and our families

—Dr Don Stammer
Economist and journalist, *The Australian* and *BRW* magazine

Contents

About the author xi

Part I: the household debt explosion 1

Part II: first things first 11

1   Work out how far in the red you are   13
2   Compare debts with income   14
3   Work out your total loan repayment bill   16
4   Get the facts on all your loans   17
5   Check your interest rates   19
6   Add up all those extra fees and charges   20
7   Sort your debts   21
8   Prioritise your debts   24
9   Check your credit rating   26
10   Make a calendar and set targets   27

Part III: mortgages   29

11   Do the numbers   31

12   Increase your mortgage repayments   34

13   Make one-off extra payments   37

14   Use pay rises to increase your loan repayments   41

15   Shorten the life of the loan   43

16   Use your income patterns to pay off sooner   45

17   Pay fortnightly instead of monthly   47

18   Shop around for a lower rate   48

19   Keep repayments flat when rates fall   51

20   Don't keep switching loans   53

21   When refinancing, stick with your existing lender
     if you can   55

22   Always choose principal-and-interest loans over
     interest-only loans   56

23   Stick with floating mortgages   58

24   Avoid redraw mortgages   60

25   Be careful of offset accounts   62

26   Don't use line-of-credit mortgages   64

27   Beware the honeymoon rate nightmare   66

28   Don't capitalise loans   68

29   Upgrade your subprime loan   71

30   Consolidate debt at your peril!   72

31   Don't pay for features you don't need   75

32   Take into account all fees   77

33   All fees are negotiable   79

34   Don't count on your partner's income to borrow more   80

35   Mortgage brokers—spot the double take   82

36   Check that you are getting the correct rate changes   84

37   Let a tenant pay the mortgage   85

Contents

38 Consider long-term house-sitting 86

39 Plan a mortgage-burning party in advance 88

40 Pay off the mortgage before investing 89

41 Don't bank on your superannuation fund to pay
    off the mortgage 93

42 Let grown-up kids pay part of your mortgage 94

43 Consider mortgage contributions instead of presents 95

44 Downsize — smaller house, smaller mortgage 96

45 Trade up houses, but trade down debt 98

46 Try the payout two-step 101

47 Avoid complex mortgage-reduction schemes 102

48 If you have to sell, stay in control 103

Part IV: credit cards 105

49 Find out how much you spend on credit cards 107

50 Choose the right card for your needs 108

51 Avoid credit card surfing 108

52 Never use cash advances 109

53 Cut up your store cards 110

54 Never pay just the minimum amount 111

55 Keep payments flat 113

56 Use direct debits 114

57 Check every item on statements 115

58 Once you've paid it off, cut it up 116

59 Consider changing to charge cards 117

60 If you have a charge card, don't take up the
    credit option 118

61 Reduce your credit limits 119

62 Do leave home without it! 120

Part V: car loans, personal loans, boat loans and store loans 123

63 Renegotiate, don't refinance 125

64 Always pay a cash deposit 126

65 Never buy new 128

66 Don't self-insure 130

67 Don't use store loans 131

68 If you fall into arrears, tell your lender as soon as possible 132

69 Get the credit bureau to limit more lending 134

70 Celebrate each win 135

Part VI: investment loans 137

71 Use principal-and-interest loans for investment properties 139

72 Avoid fixed-rate loans for rental properties 140

73 Avoid lines of credit for investment properties 141

74 Use your tax refund 142

75 Don't use deposit bonds 143

76 Don't borrow for the holiday house 145

77 Borrow in the same currency as your income 146

78 Beware the margin on share loans 149

79 Use dividends to pay off the principal on share loans 151

Part VII: small business debts 153

80 Get your personal finances sorted before starting a business 155

81 Keep business finances separate 156

82 Use your business plan 156

83 Don't make capital purchases using the overdraft 157

Contents

84 Don't extend your lease term too long   158

85 Avoid high lease residuals   160

86 When buying a business, do your research   161

87 Don't borrow to buy a franchise   163

88 Be careful of line-of-credit mortgages for business   164

89 Use supplier terms and customer terms sensibly   165

90 Sell your debtors   167

91 Maximise depreciation   168

92 Never pay full price for business equipment   170

93 Business succession to reduce debt   171

Part VIII: avoiding and minimising debt   173

94 Maintain an emergency cash fund   175

95 Use separate accounts for savings goals   176

96 No deposit, no mortgage   177

97 Renters, get a 10 to 15 per cent discount on
    your first home   179

98 Don't borrow to put money into superannuation   181

99 Avoid tax-based schemes   182

100 Be careful if guaranteeing other people's debts   183

101 Beware the lender who says you can afford a loan   185

Part IX: the final pay-off   189

Part X: useful resources   191

Index   195

About the author

Ashley Ormond was one of Australia's first PC-equipped 'mobile lenders', starting out in the early 1980s with a financial calculator, a dual-floppy drive Compaq portable PC and a portable Epson thermal printer in his car. This was before the age of mobile phones, the internet, Windows, Excel, or even hard drives. It was back in the days when:

$ lenders actually analysed each borrower's ability to repay

$ borrowers actually had to have a job or other source of income

$ borrowers actually had to have proof of a savings record, proof of income, proof of assets

$ lenders had to actually think about how each debt would be repaid, instead of just shovelling money out the door

$ lenders actually retained the credit risk and retained the ownership of loans, instead of just selling them to unsuspecting bond-holders on the other side of the world.

His banking and finance career included several senior executive roles at major Australian and international banking and finance groups, including running branch networks, lending operations, product development, pricing and financial control. His formal qualifications include a Bachelor and Masters in Law, a Bachelor of Arts in Economic History and a Graduate Diploma in Applied Finance and Investment. He has also lectured for the Securities Institute of Australia. Since 'retiring' at 40, he has been a director of several companies, including listed, private and not-for-profit companies and a charitable foundation.

Ashley is the principal of Investing 101 Pty Ltd, a specialist investment research firm that holds an Australian Financial Services Licence. He is a sought-after speaker and commentator on financial markets and has written two best-selling books on finance: *How to Give Your Kids $1 Million Each!* and *$1 Million for Life*.

Ashley lives in Sydney with his wife and two children. He may be contacted at <ashley@investing101.com>. Visit his website for access to newsletters, updates and other useful articles: <www.investing101.com.au>.

Disclaimer

This book is intended to provide general information only, to assist readers to make their own decisions and choices. This book is intended for educational and instructional purposes only, and is not intended to constitute personal financial advice or taxation advice. It does not take into account each reader's individual objectives, financial situation or needs. Readers should obtain their own financial, tax and legal advice to determine whether the information contained in this book is appropriate to their particular objectives, financial situation and needs.

The author is the principal, owner and authorised representative of Investing 101 Pty Ltd, which holds Australian Financial Services Licence 301808 issued by the Australian Securities and Investments Commission under section 913B of the *Corporations Act 2001*. Neither the author or any related company or entity receives any fees, commissions nor any other benefits from any product provider. Nor are they involved in selling or promoting any seminars, courses, trading systems or marketing schemes. A current financial services guide is available from <www.investing101.com.au>.

Part I

The household debt explosion

Between 1992 and 2008, Australians experienced a 17-year-long economic boom that handed us a golden opportunity to get into financial shape — but we blew it. With an unprecedented run of uninterrupted economic growth following the 1990–91 recession until the 2008 credit crisis, we had the best-performing economy in the Western world. During this time we enjoyed rising incomes, stable government, no major wars and low unemployment, interest rates, inflation and oil prices. Despite this lengthy period of superb economic conditions, we didn't get our houses in order. Instead, we went on a debt-fuelled spending binge:

$ housing debts grew by 800 per cent, or 14 per cent compound per year

$ non-housing personal debts grew by 260 per cent, or 8 per cent compound per year

$ credit card debts grew by nearly 1000 per cent, or 15 per cent compound per year.

(Source: Reserve Bank of Australia, Lending and Credit Aggregates table—D02, RBA, Canberra)

We borrowed more and more, saved less and less, and continued down the same path of increased spending and borrowing that we have been following since the 1970s (see figure 1.1).

Figure 1.1: Australian household debts and savings ratios

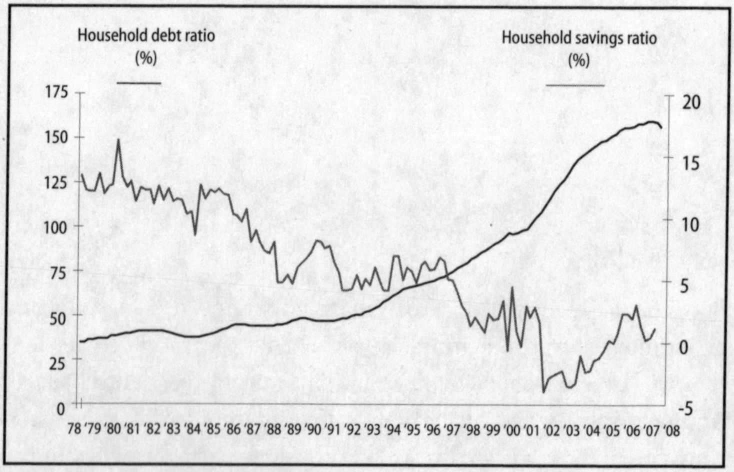

Source: Reserve Bank of Australia, tables B12 and B21.

All this occurred at a time when, according to the Australian Bureau of Statistics, total salaries and wages grew by less than

6 per cent per year, inflation ran at less than 3 per cent per year and the population grew by just 1 per cent per year. The corporate sector cleaned up its act and reduced debt levels, and the federal government got out of debt and into surplus. But the household sector, which makes up two-thirds of the overall economy, loaded up on debt and spent as if there was no tomorrow! If fact, for most of the 2000s Australia had a *negative* household savings rate, meaning we spent more than we earned. We kept on spending even though our wallets, purses and bank accounts were empty—and we borrowed even more to make up the difference.

Australia's and New Zealand's performance on the household finances front are just about the worst in the world. Our levels of household debt are even higher than the US and UK where the 2008–09 credit crisis hit hardest, and our debts have been growing at a faster rate than almost any other country (see figure 1.2).

Figure 1.2: worldwide household debt as percentage of disposable incomes

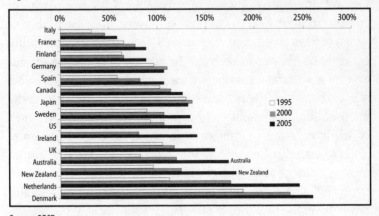

Source: OECD

We are among the worst savers in the world. Over the 30 years leading up to the 2008–09 economy crisis, we had been saving less and less of our income, and now the only countries with worse household savings rates are Greece and Estonia (see figure 1.3).

Figure 1.3: household savings as a percentage of disposable incomes

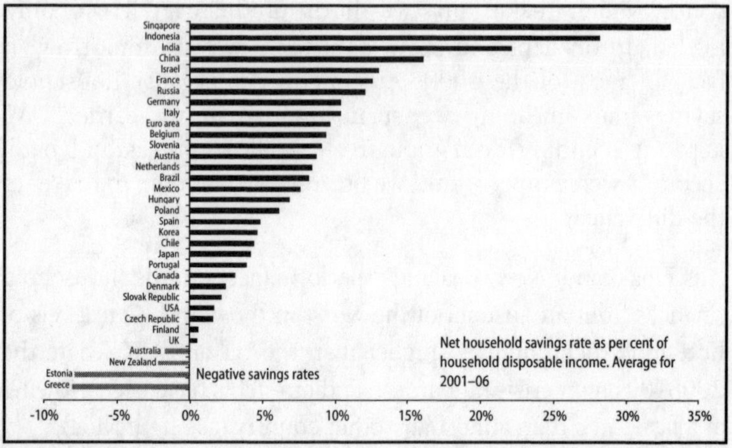

Singapore
Indonesia
India
China
Israel
France
Russia
Germany
Italy
Euro area
Belgium
Slovenia
Austria
Netherlands
Brazil
Mexico
Hungary
Poland
Spain
Korea
Chile
Japan
Portugal
Canada
Denmark
Slovak Republic
USA
Czech Republic
Finland
UK
Australia
New Zealand
Estonia
Greece

Negative savings rates

Net household savings rate as per cent of household disposable income. Average for 2001–06

-10%   -5%   0%   5%   10%   15%   20%   25%   30%   35%

Source: OECD

Our nil or negative savings rate, together with our persistent current account deficits, means we haven't even been able to generate the investment required to provide jobs for future generations. We need to rely on the savings of foreigners for our economic welfare. A country with a current account deficit is like a household that spends more than it earns. In order to make up the difference it must either borrow more from foreigners or sell more assets to foreigners. In doing so, we burden future generations with interest on the debt and we lose the future income from the assets we sell. Take a look at the top countries in figure 1.3. They have been powering ahead and building wealth rapidly over the past couple of decades, while those at the bottom have had to rely on the crumbs from their banquet.

Over the past decade the world went on a debt-fuelled consumer spending spree and Australians were the worst offenders. We were hypnotised by a string of unrealistic assumptions that turned out to be false:

- $ house prices would never fall (they do)
- $ share prices would keep rising forever (they don't)
- $ China and India would somehow be 'uncoupled' from the rest of the world and keep commodity prices high (they didn't)
- $ inflation and interest rates would never rise (they do).

Lenders abandoned basic lending rules and consumers abandoned common sense. Now the party's over and we're left with a mountain of debt. Our retirement funds in the superannuation system have been growing over the same period, but we can't rely on this to get us out of debt and fund our retirements as well. The 'superannuation revolution' has been more than wiped out by the household debt explosion. On a net basis we're actually no better off than before the compulsory superannuation system started 20 years ago, because household debts have risen faster and further than superannuation fund balances (see figure 1.4). We need to get out of debt—fast.

Figure 1.4: Australian household debts and superannuation fund balances

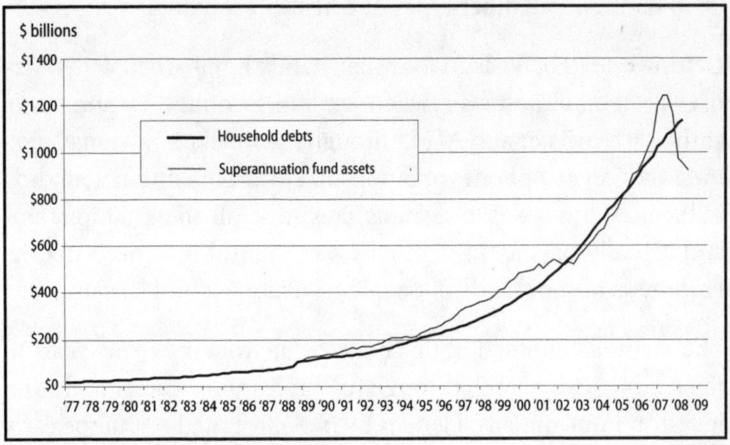

Source: Reserve Bank of Australia, tables B18 and D02.

Having high levels of household debt is dangerous at a national level and for each household. High debts make us vulnerable to economic shocks such as rising interest rates and unemployment, as well as falling incomes, house prices and asset values.

High debts also mean we are not financially independent; rather, we are at the mercy of lenders and reliant on others for our financial wellbeing. The sooner we get out of debt the sooner we can get on with building real wealth for the future—for our retirement and for our families. Having no debt means having more control over our lives and more flexibility—to not have to work just to pay the mortgage and other debts, and to be able to decide for ourselves when we want to work less, retire, travel, study or take a break. Having no debts also means less stress and less worry, and that means a healthier and more enjoyable life.

Getting out of debt is not just a good idea in recessions. Having no personal debt is one of the fundamental principles of building wealth. Personal debts comprise all debts that aren't used to generate investment or business income. These include home mortgages, credit cards, personal loans, lines of credit, car loans, boat loans and all other types of consumer lending.

Getting into debt is easy. We are constantly bombarded with offers of easy credit almost everywhere we look—on the TV and radio, at the cash register and ATM, through the mailbox, via email, text messages on our phones and pop-up ads on the internet, and on billboards, bus sides and trains. Resisting all these temptations and actually paying off debt may seem hard but it need not be. Hundreds of thousands of people have done it and so can you.

The methods outlined in this book come from my many years in the lending game, both through my professional career and as an investor. I was initially a lender by trade. I started out in the early 1980s as a lender and spent many years in major Australian and international banking groups. I have seen the lending game from all angles—from lending to consumers and small businesses to major corporations and everything in between. My time in the banking system included several senior executive roles, from running branch networks, developing products and systems, and running marketing departments, to being chairman of the pricing committee and chief financial officer of one of the 'big four' retail banks in Australia. I have consulted to mortgage brokers and originators. Over the years I have also built, bought and sold a number of businesses, and advised business owners and companies on financial structure and raising capital.

Although my wife and I made good incomes while we were working, we have made most of our money from our investments, mainly in properties and shares. We discovered early on that working pays the bills but it doesn't build wealth—only investing builds wealth.

In the case of our properties, we started out in 1986 with a mortgage on our first house, then we watched in horror as our mortgage interest rate shot up to 18 per cent by the end of 1989. This was all the motivation we needed to put everything into paying it off over the next few years. Since then we have bought many properties of all shapes and sizes, and we have used—and paid off—a number of different types of mortgages from a variety of lenders. Our properties have contributed about half of our total wealth (the other half has been from shares).

Having to pay off an 18 per cent mortgage while heading into the 1990–91 recession also taught us some critical lessons, such as spend less than we earn, always pay credit cards off in full each month, and always pay cash for items that depreciate in value (for example, furniture, cars, holidays, boats and renovations). These are lessons we have followed ever since. Fortunately we were able to retire from 'work' several years ago and live off our investments while our two kids were still young.

About this book

I have seen many people use debt wisely to make a lot of money, but I have also seen many people get into trouble with debt because they didn't know how to use it properly. They let debt control them instead of the other way around. This book provides you with an insider's knowledge of how to beat the lenders at their own game.

This is not a self-help book full of New-Age mumbo jumbo and nonsense such as 'Just think positive thoughts and the universe will provide!' or 'Dream of a dollar figure and it will magically appear in your bank account!' This book is very different. It outlines dozens of practical and proven methods that just about anybody can use to get out of debt and stay out of debt. It covers the major types of personal debt. It also covers small business debts and investment debts as nearly one-third of Australian adults either operate a small business or own investment properties or shares bought with debt.

Building wealth is not about earning more money, because higher incomes usually just disappear in higher expenses. Building wealth is about what you do with the money you have. To pay off debts and start building wealth you need to change what you do with your money. There are dozens of practical things virtually anybody can do to reduce spending to free up cash, but these are beyond the scope of this book. There are many books and websites full of great ideas on budgeting and spending less. This book is about how to put money to its best use to get out of debt as quickly and as effectively as possible.

Often people know they can change their habits and they know what to do, but they don't know where to start and are put off by the sheer size of the problem: perhaps a 30-year, $500 000 mortgage; or maybe a $20 000 credit card bill that won't budge;

or a line of credit that keeps creeping up instead of down. It's a little like the smoker who says, 'I can quit any time' or the dieter who says, 'I can always start tomorrow'. They probably can but they don't.

The aim of this book is to show that there are many practical and proven ways to make real progress towards getting out of debt and on the path to wealth, no matter how big or how complex the problem may seem. I hope this book provides a spark that spurs you into getting started.

I wish you all the best in your quest to win the war on debt.

Ashley Ormond
March 2009

Part II

First things first

The first step on any journey is to find out where you stand right now. This means getting a picture of your current debt position and putting together a plan of action to attack the problem.

1 Work out how far in the red you are

Most people don't know how much they owe in total. They usually have some idea about how much they owe on the main loans, such as the mortgage and car loan, but get a nasty surprise when they add up the grand total of all their debts.

The first step is to write down what you think the total amount of all your debts might be. Write down your initial guess on this page — now.

Next, make a list of the actual current balances outstanding on each of your loans and debts. Don't guess this time. Look up the most recent statements for each loan. These days you can access statements on most types of accounts via the internet. Include the following debts in your list:

$ home mortgages

$ investment property loans

$ amounts still owing on the construction of your house if you are building

$ lines of credit

$ credit cards

$ store cards

$ personal loans

$ car loans

$ boat loans

$ HECS-HELP (higher education loans)

$ higher purchase loans on appliances or household goods

$ rent–buy agreements on appliances, laptops, etc.

$ store loans (such as 'pay no interest for two years' loans on furniture, audio-visual and other household goods)

$ margin loans (on shares or managed funds)

$ loans to buy shares in your employer's company (including employee share purchase plans)

$ loans to friends and family

$ any loans or debts you have guaranteed

$ taxes payable

$ all bills outstanding (such as phone, electricity and water)

$ court judgements against you.

Once you have added up the total debt figure, write it down next to your initial guess. How close were you to your guess?

2 Compare debts with income

What is even more important than the total amount of your debt is how it compares with the amount of income you earn. For example, consider two families, the Joneses and the Davies. The Jones family owes $200 000 but earns $200 000 per year after tax, whereas the Davies family owes $100 000 but earns only $50 000 per year after tax. Even though the Davies family has less overall debt, they will take a lot longer to get rid of their debts because their income is much lower than the Joneses.

Work out your after-tax income per year. Include all sources of regular income like overtime, part-time or casual work. Use recent pay slips to calculate the total after-tax income for one year. Next, work out how many years of after-tax income your total debts represent by dividing your total debt by your annual after-tax income.

For example, if your total debts are \$240 000 and your total annual after-tax income is \$85 000, then your debts equal 2.8 times your annual income. This does not mean that it will take 2.8 years to pay off all your debts because it doesn't include your living expenses and interest on the debts, but it is a good, quick measure of the seriousness of your debt burden.

As a nation, Australian households had a debt-to-income ratio of 1.6 at the end of 2008, but it had risen from just 0.8 over the past 10 years. See table 2.1 to find out how you rate. (Your debt-to-income ratio is your total debts divided by your annual after-tax income.)

Table 2.1: debt-to-income ratios

Debt-to-income ratio	What it means	Action needed
0	Debt free already!	Relax — keep it this way
0–1	Moderate level of debt	The end is in sight! Set a goal to get rid of the last bit of debt, then celebrate!
1–2	High level of debt	Keep paying off existing debt and avoid new debts
2–3	Very high level of debt	Accelerate action to get the debt under control
More than 3	Extreme level of debt. Very highly vulnerable to adverse changes in circumstances, such as loss of income and rises in interest rates. You're heavily reliant on a good economy and the goodwill of lenders.	Take radical action to attack the level of debt *urgently*

3 Work out your total loan repayment bill

Most people also get a rude shock when they work out what all their debts are costing them in total repayments. Once again, make a quick mental guess as to the total of all loan repayments on all your debts each year. Write your guess down now, then complete the following steps.

- $ Add up the total repayments (including principal and interest) on all your loans (get the actual numbers from recent statements). For lines of credit and credit cards, use the minimum payment amount or the amount you have been paying if it is above the minimum level.

- $ Add all fees on loans, then add these to the total repayments. Include all fees—administration fees, service fees, late-payment fees, statement fees, transaction fees and cash advance fees—they all add up.

- $ Divide the total annual loan payments (including all the above items) by your total annual after-tax income. This will give you your debt-service ratio, which is the percentage of your after-tax income required to service (or repay) your debts.

For example, if your total loan repayments (including principal, interest, fees and charges on all loans) add up to $2100 per month, your annual bill is $25200 per year. If you earn $70000 after tax per year, your debt-service ratio is 36 per cent; that is, 36 per cent of your after-tax income is going to pay off debts.

Before the recent lending boom, a debt-service ratio of more than 30 per cent of income was considered excessive and dangerous, and lenders would limit the amount of lending so that 30 per cent would not be exceeded. However, over the past decade, this rule was relaxed and many borrowers have total repayments above 50 per cent of their income, which is extremely dangerous. Table 2.2 shows how you rate.

Table 2.2: debt-service ratios

Debt-service ratio	What it means	Action needed
Below 15%	Low	Use surplus cash to get rid of debt as soon as possible
15–30%	Moderate	Keep paying off existing debt and avoid new debts
30–50%	High — dangerous level of debt	Accelerate action to get the debt under control
More than 50%	Extreme — lenders should never let you get into this position	Take radical action to attack the level of debt *urgently*

4 Get the facts on all your loans

Before working out a plan to pay off your debts, you need to find out how they all work. Some information may be obtained from loan statements, but usually you need to call the lender to get all the facts. For each loan, find out the following information:

$ current balance and payout figure (which includes payout fees and charges)

$ term remaining—get the date of the final payment

$ whether there is any lump sum due at the end of the term (often called a balloon or bullet payment)

$ current interest rate

$ how the interest is calculated; for example, is it calculated on the daily balance, the minimum monthly balance, the maximum monthly balance, the end of month balance or the opening monthly balance.

$ what ongoing fees are payable, including monthly, annual and statement fees

$ whether the interest rate is fixed for the term of the loan or floating (variable); if fixed, for how long is it fixed?

$ whether the payments are principal-and-interest or interest only

$ what the lender's security for the loan is

$ who the borrowers on the loan are, and whether there are any guarantors

$ what happens if you make additional payments or higher payments than the regular payments. On some types of loan (many car loans, personal loans and some mortgages) extra payments aren't used to reduce the principal, but just put the loan into 'advance'. Putting the loan into advance doesn't reduce your interest bill, it just gives the lender free use of the extra money, which is of no benefit to you

$ what the penalties and fees for early repayment of the loan are

$ what the fees involved in changing the term and repayments are

$ where the repayments come from; are they automatic debits from other accounts or your payroll, or manual payments?

$ whether the loan automatically converts (or rolls over) to a new loan at a specified date. For example, some mortgages automatically convert from interest only to principal-and-interest after an initial period such as two or three years.

5 Check your interest rates

Many borrowers are paying a different interest rate on their loan from the rate appearing on the loan statement. Usually this is not because the lender is being deliberately fraudulent (although many are). Rather, it is generally because the lender is incompetent. Large lenders and banks have extremely complex systems, and very few of their staff actually know how they work. A day doesn't go past without them finding a bug somewhere in the system.

Interest on most loans is calculated on the daily balance and the interest is debited monthly. First, check the interest calculations. For example, for a 7 per cent mortgage with a balance of $100 000, the monthly interest bill should be:

$ for a 31-day month: $100 000 × 7% ÷ 365 × 31 = $594.52

$ for a 30-day month: $100 000 × 7% ÷ 365 × 30 = $575.34

Some lenders average the number of days out over the year and calculate interest for each month at 30.417 days per month. You may find that your lender uses 31 days each month, in which case they are stealing an extra week's interest from you each year.

If the interest debited each month doesn't match your calculations, ring the lender and ask him or her how it is calculated. It may take a few phone calls before you find someone who actually knows how their system works.

Next, check that the principal balance is reducing in the correct way. For example, if your repayments are $700 per month on the above loan, for a 31-day month, $594.52 should be interest (see above) and the balance of $105.48 ($700.00 – $594.52) should be reducing the principal balance. Check that the balance is reducing by the correct amount each month on the statement.

Even if the calculations are correct this is a great exercise to help you understand how your loan works and where your repayments actually go.

6 Add up all those extra fees and charges

Interest is only one way lenders make money from you. Almost all lenders charge extra fees and charges for almost all types of loans. There are many types of fees and charges, including:

$ front-end fees (at the start of the loan), such as application fees, approval fees and settlement fees. In the old days before computers, humans manually assessed your loan so there was a cost involved. These days almost all consumer loans (including mortgages) are processed and approved by computers in seconds and the costs are only a few cents, not hundreds of dollars

$ ongoing fees, such as annual fees and monthly fees. They are called a variety of names, including administration fees, servicing fees, processing fees, statement fees and transaction fees

$ back-end fees (at the end of the loan), such as payout fees, exit fees, settlement fees and termination fees. In some cases excess payout fees are illegal, so lenders simply call them deferred establishment fees instead to get around the law

$ ad-hoc fees, such as fees for renegotiating terms of the loan, penalty interest fees, late payment fees, lump sum repayment fees, processing fees, arrears fees, collection fees, transaction fees, and fees for changing the frequency of payments (for example, switching from monthly to fortnightly payments).

All these fees bear no relation to the costs incurred by the lender. Almost all handling and processing of loans these days is electronic. Fees and charges are simply ways of getting more money out of your pocket and into the lender's pocket, in order to make the stated interest rate appear lower than it really is.

Get hold of the past year's statements of each of your loans and add up all the extra fees and charges for a whole year. If you don't keep loan statements, start doing it now. Checking loan statements is a good habit to get into, so you can check your progress on getting out of debt. For many types of loans you can download past statements and transaction histories free from the lenders' websites.

7   Sort your debts

Not all debts are created equal. Mortgages are a necessary evil (because it's virtually impossible to buy your first house without one), but mortgages on your subsequent houses and all other types of personal debts are just plain evil and should be banished forever as soon as possible. Generally the best kind of debts are:

$ where the asset bought with the debt generates income and/or grows in value in excess of the loan interest rate

$ where the interest is tax deductible, which usually occurs when the asset bought with the debt generates taxable income.

Examples include debts used to buy investments or to fund a business where the profits and/or growth in value exceed the interest rate on the debt. Also included here are debts to pay for education and training that increase your future income by more than the cost of the course and the interest.

The worst kind of debt is used to buy items that either depreciate in value (such as cars) or have no monetary value at all (such as living expenses or holidays). These types of debt carry the highest interest rates and the interest is not tax deductible. Table 2.3 is a summary of the various kinds of household debt.

Table 2.3: different types of household debt

	Items bought with debt	Tax-deductible interest?	Value appreciates or depreciates?	Good or bad?
Good debts	Investment	Yes	Value appreciates over long term	Good, but select wisely
	Own business	Yes	Value appreciates as profits grow	Good, but high risk of failure
	Education and training	Some	Generates future income	Good, but ensure there is clear link to future income
Undesire- able but necessary debts	Your home	No	Land appreciates (if well located, the land value can appreciate at a higher rate than loan interest rate)	Okay, but pay it off quickly
	Home renovations	No	Value depreciates — need to sell quickly to get value back	Usually bad, as items depreciate. Only okay if you sell immediately when finished

	Items bought with debt	Tax deductible interest?	Value appreciates or depreciates?	Good or bad?
Bad debts	Personal and household items	No	Value depreciates rapidly	Bad — never do it
	Living expenses	No	No monetary value	Bad — never do it

I don't regard a home mortgage as 'good debt' in most cases. The reason is that when you buy a home you are really buying two things. Part of the value of the property is in the *land*, and the other part is in the *improvements*, which is the buildings and everything in them, including concrete, bricks and mortar, timber, roof tiles, floors and appliances. The land part of the property can *increase* in value, depending on its location and the supply and demand for land in that area. If the location is strong — for example if it is close to transport, schools, shops and recreational facilities, or has good views — then the land can increase in value at two to three percentage points above the inflation rate over the long term. It needs to do this because mortgage interest rates are also about two to three percentage points above the inflation rate.

The problem is that the improvements on the land always decrease in value over time because they need constant repairs and maintenance, they go out of fashion, fail to keep up with the needs of modern life and eventually need replacing. In most residential properties, especially in outer suburbs far from transport, employment and services, where the potential for land value appreciation is lowest and improvements make up a large part of the overall purchase price, the overall value of the property won't increase over the long term at a rate higher than the interest rate on mortgages used to buy it.

The second reason I don't like calling a mortgage 'good' debt is that I have seen too many people fall into the trap of increasing their mortgage to put all kinds of things such as cars, boats and holidays 'on the mortgage', and simply say 'It must be okay because a mortgage is a good debt, isn't it?' All this does is keep them in debt for years longer than necessary.

Borrowing to buy a *first* home is okay because it is the only way to get into the property market initially, but pay it off as soon as you can, so you can start building equity in the house and ultimately become debt free. After the first home, all subsequent houses you buy to live in should be paid for in cash.

Renovations always depreciate over time. Remember—only the *land* component of a home appreciates in value, but the *improvements* always depreciate. Further, most renovations don't add value in excess of their cost. A renovation should really be considered a lifestyle expense, not an investment, so you should not borrow unless you can pay it off very quickly or sell soon after the renovations are done, while they are still new.

8   Prioritise your debts

The number one priority is to pay all bills that are in arrears (or past due), especially where there is a risk of your electricity or water being cut off, your car being repossessed or of you being evicted.

Once the arrears are under control, the general rule is that it is always best to pay off debts with the highest effective cost (including interest rates and fees less any tax deduction for interest, if any) first. The most expensive debts are unsecured personal debts (where the lender takes no security) such as credit cards, store loans (those 'buy now pay no interest for two years' loans for household items), personal lines of credit and personal loans. Once fees are added, the interest rates on these loans are generally between 20 and 30 per cent per year. Attack these first.

Once these are paid off, the next most expensive category of debts are those secured by depreciating assets, such as cars, boats, furniture and other household items. Interest rates on these types of loans are generally around 10 to 20 per cent—that is, lower than unsecured debts—because the lender has some security it can repossess and sell if you default on the loan. If there is still a shortfall after the lender sells the item and take the proceeds, the lender can chase you for the rest.

Once these types of debts are paid off completely, the next category to attack is your debts secured by real estate that don't generate income. This category includes home mortgages, line of credit mortgages and the like.

Finally, the last category to attack is debts with tax-deductible interest. These include investment property loans, margin loans, business leases, business overdrafts and other business loans. Debt used to generate business and investment income is good debt and can help build wealth if it generates income or growth in excess of the interest rate. But the ultimate aim is still to pay off these debts to maximise your wealth and financial freedom.

Rather than trying to pay off several debts at once, it is usually best to put every effort into paying off one debt at a time. This way you can really focus your attention on one clear goal and you can celebrate when you achieve the goal. You still need to make the regular payments on each of your debts but, beyond that, focus on using extra cash to pay off one debt at a time.

9   Check your credit rating

Whenever you apply for a loan, whether it's a mortgage, car loan, personal loan, credit card or store loan, the lender will check with a credit rating agency to see what is on your file. What the lender finds there will go a long way towards determining whether the loan is approved and, if so, what interest rate you pay.

The main consumer credit agency in Australia is Veda Advantage Ltd and it has files on more than 13 million Australian and New Zealand borrowers. Your file contains a huge amount of personal information, including:

$ personal details such as name, residential addresses, date of birth, driver's licence number, and current and/or previous employer

$ all credit applications and enquiries you have made during the past five years

$ records of current credit accounts

$ overdue accounts (defaults) that may have been listed against your name

$ information on the public record including Bankruptcy Act information, court judgements, writs and summons, directorships and proprietorships.

Many people are paying higher interest rates than they should because their credit rating contains incorrect or out-of-date information. All sorts of things can end up on your file even if you think they have been sorted out, including disputes over phone bills, electricity bills and rent. If the dispute has been solved and you were not at fault, apply to have it removed from your credit file. There have also been numerous cases of mistaken identity, where a borrower ends up paying for somebody else's credit mistakes, because somehow the data ends up on the wrong file.

Order a copy of your file today. This can be done online for a small fee, or you can have it mailed to you at no cost. Make sure you get the credit agency to correct any errors. Then check the file again every year until all your debts are cleared.

The contact details are:

$ Australia: < www.mycreditfile.com.au>
Phone: 1300 762 207

$ New Zealand: <www.mycreditfile.co.nz>
Phone: 0800 692 733

10 Make a calendar and set targets

Most people want to get out of debt, but fail to make real progress because they don't have a detailed action plan. There is nothing like writing down specific targets and dates to really get an action plan under way.

Set up two calendars:

1 The first calendar is for the short term—the next 12 months. List each of your debts in order of priority, starting with the highest priority on top, and write the current balance against each. Next, draw columns across the page for each month or quarter during the year. In each column for each month or quarter, write down a specific target balance for each debt. Some debts you will probably aim to pay off in a few months (such as credit cards), and others (such as the mortgage) will reduce from the current balance as you make the normal repayments. At the bottom of each column put the total debt target for each month or quarter, so you can see your total debt reducing over time.

2   The second calendar is for the long term, say five or
    10 years, to pay off all debts completely. Draw columns for
    each year across the page and write target balances for each
    year column for each loan. At the bottom of each column
    add up the total debt target per year.

Make sure you check the plan each month or quarter and update
the balances from your loan statements.

If you are not staying on track make sure you find out why. It
may be because the interest rates on your variable rate loans have
changed, or it may be because you overestimated the amount
of spare cash you were able to put into the loans to reduce the
principal. Reassess the plan each year and revise your targets for
each debt.

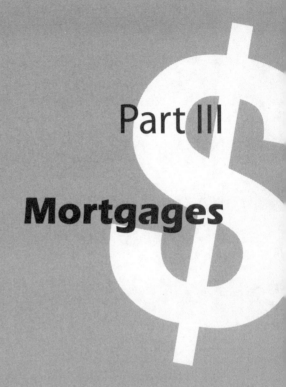

Part III

Mortgages

A home mortgage is the largest debt you will be likely to take on in your life, and it is usually the debt that lasts the longest, so it is the largest section of this book. A home mortgage is a necessary evil because it is usually the only way to buy a first home. From there the aim should be to get rid of it as quickly as possible, so you can get on with building real wealth.

Every dollar you spend on mortgage payments is two dollars you could be investing instead to build wealth for the future, thanks to the numerous tax breaks you get for investing.

Although a mortgage might start out at several hundred thousand dollars over 25 or 30 years, there are dozens of ways that can help you pay it off much sooner.

11 Do the numbers

Most of your repayments go towards paying interest to the lender, and in most cases less than half of your total repayments actually go towards paying back the amount borrowed (the loan principal). For example, if you borrow $300 000 over 25 years at 7 per cent, you end up paying back a total of $636 101 (not counting fees and other charges), which is more than double the amount you borrowed in the first place.

Table 3.1 shows the situation for loans at interest rates of 5 per cent, 7 per cent and 10 per cent when $300 000 is borrowed over 25 years.

Table 3.1: mortgage repayments for different interest rates when $300 000 is borrowed over 25 years

Interest rate	5%	7%	10%
Repayments per month	$1 753.77	$2 120.34	$2 726.10
Total repayments	$526 131.04	$636 101.28	$817 830.67
Principal repaid	$300 000.00	$300 000.00	$300 000.00
Interest paid	$226 131.04	$336 101.28	$517 830.67
Interest as % of total repayments	43%	53%	63%

The next important factor is that the loan balance reduces very slowly at the start of the loan, because in the early years the majority of each repayment goes towards paying interest to the lender and only a very small part actually reduces your principal balance. The higher the interest rate, the greater proportion of each payment goes in interest and the slower the balance reduces over time. This can be seen in figure 3.1 (overleaf).

Figure 3.1: mortgage balance reduction at different interest rates

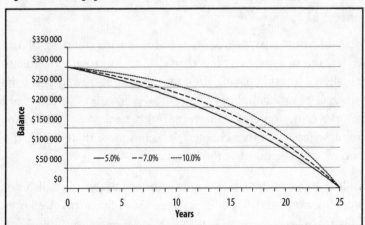

Many people get a shock when they find out how much they still owe on their mortgage after they have been paying it off for years. For example, for a 7 per cent mortgage over 25 years, after five years (or 20 per cent of the total term) you might expect that about 20 per cent of the loan would have been paid off. Wrong! After 20 per cent of the loan term, you will have paid off only 9 per cent of the loan and you still owe 91 per cent of it! Even after half the loan term (12.5 years), you have paid off only 29 per cent of the loan and you still owe 71 per cent! It may seem unfair but that's how the numbers work. All principal-and-interest mortgages work this way.

Table 3.2 sets out loan balances at various stages, at different interest rates. The higher the interest rate is, the slower the balance reduces over time and the more you owe at any stage during the loan.

Table 3.2: how a 25-year, $300 000 loan reduces over time at different interest rates

Interest rate	5.00%	7.00%	10.00%
5 years	$265 741	$273 486	$282 491
10 years	$221 773	$235 900	$253 684
15 years	$165 348	$182 617	$206 287
20 years	$92 934	$107 081	$128 305
25 years	$0	$0	$0

If you currently have a mortgage, you should complete the following exercise:

Work out how much you have paid to the lender so far by multiplying your monthly payment by the number of payments you have already made:

I have already paid: _____ per month × _____ months paid = $ _____

If your repayments have changed since you took out the loan, still add up the total you have paid so far.

Next, see how much has come off the loan principal by comparing the current loan balance with the amount you initially borrowed plus any additional amounts borrowed.

Amount I have paid off the principal:

Initial loan of: _____ minus current balance of : _____ total amount borrowed = $ _____

Finally, work out how much you are contracted to pay in the future by multiplying the monthly payment by the number of months remaining in the term.

I still owe: _____ per month × _____ months left = $ _____

If you have an interest-only loan you need to add the principal onto the total amount payable because you will still owe this at the end of the loan term.

If these results don't scare you into action, then nothing will. This exercise drives home the importance of getting a low interest rate on your loan and paying off as much as possible as early as possible to minimise the interest payable and to get rid of your debt sooner.

12 Increase your mortgage repayments

One of the most powerful ways to pay off the mortgage faster is to increase your regular monthly mortgage repayments. Even a small increase in your monthly payments can dramatically reduce the total interest bill and get rid of it sooner.

For example, for a typical $300 000 mortgage at 7 per cent over 25 years, the monthly repayments would be $2120.34. If you increased your monthly repayment amount by just $100 per month (or a little over $3 per day), you would reduce your total interest paid by 13 per cent, saving more than $43 000 in interest, and you would pay off the loan 2.7 years sooner. So, by chipping in an extra $3 per day you save $43 000 and you will be out of debt nearly three years earlier!

If you can manage to pay $400 per month (about $13 per day) more than the standard repayments you reduce your total interest paid by 36 per cent, saving you more than $122 000. You would pay off the debt nearly eight years sooner. Figure 3.2 shows how the mortgage balance reduces compared with a standard mortgage with the regular payments.

Figure 3.2: increase mortgage repayments by a fixed dollar amount

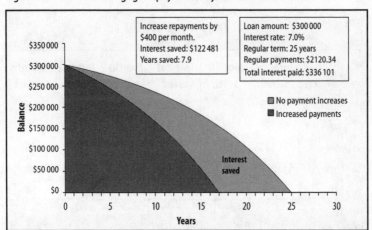

Even if you increase your repayments by just $1 per day you can save $15 000 and cut almost a year off the average mortgage term. Not bad for just $1 per day! Imagine getting out of debt a whole year earlier by spending just $1 per day. That's a whole year that you can put the money towards your investment plan, instead of still paying off the mortgage. Looked at another way, by spending just $1 per day starting now you can retire a year earlier! Surely everybody can do this.

If you don't think that you can increase your loan repayment, think back to when you took out the loan. If it was a few years ago your income was probably less back then, but you managed to make the repayments. In the years since the start of the loan, your income probably increased slightly each year or so, but the extra money was just spent on everyday expenses. If you are really serious about paying off the mortgage sooner, you will find out where this extra money goes and find ways of putting some of it into the mortgage instead.

Table 3.3 (overleaf) estimates how much you can save and how much sooner you can pay off the housing loan by increasing your monthly repayments.

Table 3.3: impact of increasing regular monthly repayments*

Current interest rate	6.00%		7.00%		8.00%	
Term remaining	Interest saved	Months saved	Interest saved	Months saved	Interest saved	Months saved
10 years	$2 285	8	$2 876	8	$3 544	8
15 years	$4 299	13	$5 603	14	$7 139	16
20 years	$7 144	21	$9 611	23	$12 621	26
25 years	$11 051	31	$15 294	35	$20 602	40
30 years	$16 275	43	$23 075	50	$31 711	58

Current interest rate	9.00%		10.00%	
Term remaining	Interest saved	Months saved	Interest saved	Months saved
10 years	$4 296	9	$5 138	9
15 years	$8 939	17	$11 031	18
20 years	$16 251	29	$20 580	32
25 years	$27 125	45	$35 002	51
30 years	$42 402	67	$55 297	77

*Interest saved per 5 per cent increase in monthly repayments per $100 000 mortgage, and months saved per 5 per cent increase in payments

For example, let's say you have a $250 000 mortgage at 8 per cent for 30 years. The regular repayments are $1834 per month. Now let's assume that you increase the monthly repayments by 5 per cent, or $92 per month ($3 per day) to $1926 per month and kept them at this level. The total interest savings would be $31 711 (from the table for a $100 000 mortgage) multiplied by 2.5 (for a $250 000 mortgage) = approximately $79 000 interest saved. The term is reduced by 58 months (from the table). So, just by finding an extra $3 per day you can save $79 000 and get out of debt nearly five years sooner!

13 Make one-off extra payments

Making just one extra payment off the loan principal makes a huge difference to the overall interest paid and can cut months or even years off the mortgage. For example, you can use cash from Christmas bonuses, gifts, inheritances and tax refunds. Even small contributions make a huge difference over the term of the loan.

If you have a 25-year, $300 000 mortgage at 7 per cent, just one principal reduction of $1000 made now will save $4697 in interest over the life of the loan, and pay off the whole mortgage three months sooner. That's a massive 370 per cent tax-free return on your investment of $1000.

Table 3.4 helps you to estimate how much interest you can save and how many months sooner you can pay off the loan just by making a single one-off payment off the principal.

Table 3.4: impact of a single one-off payment off the principal*

Current interest rate	6.00%		7.00%		8.00%	
Term remaining	Interest saved	Months saved	Interest saved	Months saved	Interest saved	Months saved
10 years	$817	1.6	$1005	1.7	$1214	1.8
15 years	$1443	2.9	$1831	3.1	$2280	3.4
20 years	$2281	4.6	$2990	5.1	$3849	5.8
25 years	$3400	6.8	$4611	7.9	$6141	9.3
30 years	$4891	9.8	$6864	11.8	$9461	14.3

*Interest saved per 1 per cent in one-off principal reduction, per $100 000 mortgage, and months saved per 1 per cent principal reduction.

Table 3.4 *(cont'd)*: impact of a single one-off payment off the principal*

Current interest rate	9.00%		10.00%	
Term remaining	Interest saved	Months saved	Interest saved	Months saved
10 years	$1 443	1.9	$1 695	2.0
15 years	$2 799	3.7	$3 397	4.1
20 years	$4 885	6.5	$6 135	7.4
25 years	$8 068	10.8	$10 483	12.6
30 years	$12 855	17.2	$17 250	20.8

*Interest saved per 1 per cent in one-off principal reduction, per $100 000 mortgage, and months saved per 1 per cent principal reduction.

For example, let's say you have a $200 000 mortgage at 7 per cent with 30 years remaining. A single one-off payment off the principal of $4000 is 2 per cent of the principal balance, so the interest saving is $6864 (from table 3.4 for $100 000) × 2 (for a $200 000 mortgage) × 2 (for a 2 per cent principal reduction) = approximately $27 000 in interest saved. The term is reduced by 11.8 months (from the table) × 2 (for a 2 per cent reduction) = 24 months. So by making a single $4000 payment off the principal now, you save $27 000 and get out of debt two years sooner. Not a bad return from a single one-off investment of $4000.

Better still, if you make one additional payment off the principal each year, you can really turbo-charge your mortgage, saving much more interest and getting out of debt sooner. With a $300 000, 25-year mortgage at 7 per cent, if you make an extra payment of $1000 at the end of *each year* it saves more than $35 000 in total interest and pays off the mortgage 2.2 years earlier. If you make an extra payment of $4000 at the end of each year, it saves more than $104 000 in interest and pays off the whole mortgage nearly seven years earlier. Figure 3.3 shows what it looks like compared with a standard 25-year, $300 000 mortgage at 7 per cent.

Figure 3.3: lump sum principal reductions each year

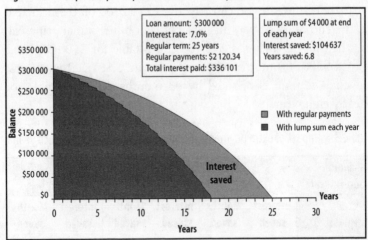

These are massive savings. Tiny amounts add up: even $100 per year can save $4000 in interest and cut two months off the term.

Before making additional repayments on your loans, ring your lender to make sure that extra payments go towards reducing the balance when interest is calculated, instead of just putting the loan into advance or in suspense. In most variable rate principal-and-interest mortgages (most home mortgages in Australia are principal and interest), extra payments do reduce your principal balance, but it always pays to ring and make sure this is the case with your loan. Then check your mortgage statements to ensure that the extra cash really did reduce the principal balance by the correct amounts.

Table 3.5 (overleaf) is a ready reckoner to help estimate how much interest you can save and how many months sooner you can pay off the loan by making an extra payment off the principal at the end of each year. It shows the interest saved per 1 per cent of principal paid each year, per $100 000 mortgage, and the months saved per 1 per cent of the principal paid each year.

Let's say you have a $200000 mortgage at 7 per cent with 30 years remaining. If you can pay an extra $2000 off the principal at the end of each year, this is 1 per cent of the initial principal, so the interest saving is $43468 (from table for $100000) × 2 (for a $200000 mortgage) = approximately $87000 in interest saved. The term is reduced by 93 months (from the table) or nearly eight years.

Table 3.5: impact of extra payments off the principal at the end of each year

Current interest rate	6.00%		7.00%		8.00%	
Term remaining	Interest saved	Months saved	Interest saved	Months saved	Interest saved	Months saved
10 years	$2987	9	$3598	9	$4247	10
15 years	$7281	16	$8912	15	$10690	15
20 years	$13829	40	$17191	42	$20937	43
25 years	$22757	64	$28649	66	$35301	69
30 years	$34203	93	$43468	93	$54029	101
Current interest rate	9.00%		10.00%			
Term remaining	Interest saved	Months saved	Interest saved	Months saved		
10 years	$4937	10	$5668	10		
15 years	$12656	18	$14755	15		
20 years	$25097	44	$29705	46		
25 years	$42762	69	$51127	75		
30 years	$65894	107	$79132	112		

Mortgages

14 Use pay rises to increase your loan repayments

One of the great advantages of borrowing to buy assets that appreciate over the long term (like well-located property, where most of the value is in the land) is that asset values and income levels tend to rise over time (mostly due to inflation), but the amount of the debt and the loan repayments do not.

As your income rises over the years, either because you are promoted, change jobs, or simply due to inflation, it is important to use part of this extra income each year to increase your mortgage repayments. Sure, part of the reason for pay rises is to compensate for the rising cost of living, but not every dollar of your pay goes to pay living expenses.

For example, if you receive a pay rise of $20 per fortnight, why don't you put $10 per fortnight into the mortgage and leave the other $10 for extra living expenses? You won't notice that the $10 per fortnight has gone into the mortgage because it is extra money you didn't have before the pay rise.

If you have a typical 25-year, $300 000 mortgage at 7 per cent and you increased your mortgage repayments by just 3 per cent each year (in line with inflation and average wages growth each year) you can save a massive $107 000 in interest and pay off the mortgage 8.6 years sooner. Figure 3.4 (overleaf) shows what making extra repayments looks like compared with leaving the repayments at their original level.

If you can increase repayments by 5 per cent each year you save $138 000 in interest and pay off the loan 11 years sooner.

Figure 3.4: effect of increasing mortgage repayments by a fixed per cent each year

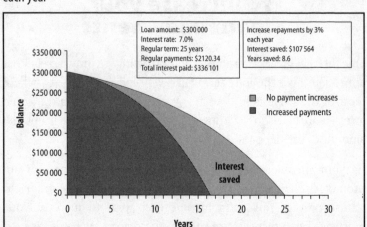

Another common source of increased cash each year is tax cuts. Nearly every year in this decade most Australians have received tax cuts. Each tax cut is a pure bonus because it comes on top of salary and wages rises. Everybody should be using at least part of the extra cash from their tax cuts to increase repayments on their debts. Unfortunately, most people spend the tax cut instead and it's gone forever.

Table 3.6 helps you estimate how much interest you can save and how many months sooner you can pay off the loan by increasing your repayments each year by just 1 per cent per year.

Imagine you have a $300 000 mortgage at 7 per cent with 20 years remaining. If you can increase your repayments by just 1 per cent each year, the interest saving is $9527 (from table for $100 000) × 3 (for a $300 000 mortgage) = approximately $28 000 in interest saved. The term is reduced by 30 months (from the table).

Table 3.6: impact of increasing repayments each year

Current interest rate	6.00%		7.00%		8.00%	
Term remaining	Interest saved	Months saved	Interest saved	Months saved	Interest saved	Months saved
10 years	$1 228	6	$1 531	6	$1 868	6
15 years	$3 437	15	$4 404	15	$5 520	16
20 years	$7 267	28	$9 527	30	$12 191	32
25 years	$13 022	42	$17 513	50	$22 738	54
30 years	$21 238	66	$28 828	77	$37 739	84
Current interest rate	9.00%		10.00%			
Term remaining	Interest saved	Months saved	Interest saved	Months saved		
10 years	$2 243	6	$2 659	6		
15 years	$6 799	17	$8 255	18		
20 years	$15 303	34	$18 904	36		
25 years	$28 885	58	$36 015	63		
30 years	$48 184	90	$60 204	97		

*Interest saved from a 1 per cent rise in repayments each year, per $100 000 mortgage, and months saved for a 1 per cent rise in repayments each year.

There's really no excuse for not increasing your repayments by at least 1 per cent each year because inflation (and wages) are rising by at least 2 or 3 per cent each year through inflation alone.

15 Shorten the life of the loan

A generation ago, most home mortgages were for terms of 20 years. Most couples married in their 20s so they paid off their 20 year loan in their 40s. This gave them another 10 or 20 years to save for their retirement once the mortgage was paid off, because most people worked into their 60s.

In the 1980s, 25-year loans became popular and in the 1990s, 30-year loans became the norm. Because many young people these days are moving out of their parents' homes later and getting married later, they are taking out 30-year loans in their 30s or 40s, which they will still be paying off in their 60s or 70s, well after they want to retire or are retrenched.

In the 2000s lending boom, some lenders even started offering loans for 40 years and even longer. (In the US there are 50 year mortgages. In Japan it is even worse: some lenders offer 100 year loans—known as 'generational loans', because the family would be paying off the loan for several generations to come!)

One so-called advantage of longer term loans is that the repayments are lower. By pushing the loan term out to a longer term, monthly repayments are reduced so you can borrow more money and buy a more expensive house. But this is all an illusion; a marketing trick by lenders to keep you in debt longer so they get more money out of you. If you are borrowing, say, $300 000 at 7 per cent over 25 years, the monthly repayments will be $2120.34. If you push the loan term out to 30 years, the repayments will be $1995.91 per month, which is 6 per cent lower. The problem is that you will end up paying $82 425 more (which is 25 per cent more) in interest over the term and you will be in debt for five years longer. So, by reducing your repayments by 6 per cent, you end up having to work five years longer to pay it off!

Don't be tempted to go for longer term loans. The rule of thumb is if you need to reduce the repayments so that the loan term goes beyond when you want to retire, then you can't afford the house. For example, if you are 30 years old now and want to retire at, say, 55, then don't go longer than a 25-year loan term so that, at worst, it is paid off by the age of 55. You don't want to be still paying off a mortgage when you're retired, and you will probably need all of your superannuation fund and retrenchment money to pay for your retirement years.

16 Use your income patterns to pay off sooner

Here's a way to use your income patterns during your various life cycle stages to pay off the mortgage sooner and save on interest.

Most young couples starting out in the housing market have two incomes in the early years before they have children. Then, while the children are young, a large proportion drop to a single income. Even if the partner continues working during this stage, the second salary is often used up in child care expenses and other related costs, so they are effectively down to a single income. Once the children are in school they often go back to a second income, although it is often lower than before, and living expenses are also higher, so we'll call it '1.5 incomes'.

If the couple took out a standard 25-year mortgage for $300 000 at 7 per cent, the repayments would remain constant at $2120.34 (apart from rising and falling variable interest rates with the ups and downs in the general economy) and they would pay a total of $336 101 in interest on top of repaying the $300 000 they originally borrowed.

A better way would be to tailor their repayments to suit the three different stages in their income. Here is one way to do it.

$ Stage 1: two incomes for five years. With two incomes, no children and no ageing parent expenses, let's say they can afford mortgage repayments of $3000 per month. They borrow $300 000 at 7 per cent with payments of $3000 per month, making the term 12.5 years.

$ Stage 2: one income for five years. At the end of the first five years, the balance will be $210 500. When young children come along and the family drops to a single income, renegotiate the loan so that the repayments are reduced to $1500 per month, making it a 24.5 year term. This stage lasts for five years while the early child care expenses are high and/or income is reduced.

$ Stage 3: 1.5 incomes. After the five years in stage 2, the balance will be $191 000. The loan is renegotiated so that payments increase to $2500, making the remaining term 8.5 years.

Under this plan, the loan is fully paid off in 18.5 years, which is 6.5 years sooner than with a standard 25-year mortgage. The total interest bill is $112 452 less than with a standard mortgage. Figure 3.5 shows the three-stage plan compared with the standard mortgage payment system.

Figure 3.5: paying off the mortgage in stages

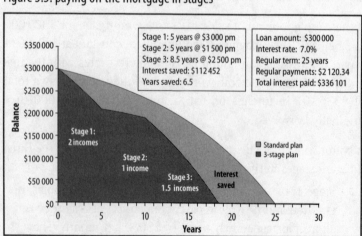

There are many ways to achieve similar results, and you can vary the stages to suit your own needs. If you currently have a variable rate principal-and-interest mortgage (which is most mortgage holders in Australia) there is no reason why you could not start out on a plan like this. It's simply a matter of having a plan, and talking to your lender and telling them what you want to achieve.

Where possible, stick with a single lender during each stage, to minimise costs. The only fee you should pay (if any) may be a renegotiation fee at the start of stages two and three. Even if you need to pay a few hundred dollars each time, this is insignificant compared with the interest saving of over $100 000.

17 Pay fortnightly instead of monthly

If you make your repayments fortnightly instead of monthly and make the fortnightly repayments half the monthly amount, you end up paying the equivalent of an extra month's payment each year. This is because there are a fraction more than two fortnights per month. These tiny fractions add up over time and can save you money.

If you are paid fortnightly, like a large proportion of people, make the fortnightly payments directly from your payroll. With a $300 000 mortgage over 25 years at 7 per cent, this will save around $70 000 in interest and cut more than four years off the mortgage. This result is achieved mainly because you are actually paying more off each year. Although it may sound difficult if you think about it as having to come up with an extra month's repayment per year, if you set up your budget so that there are two fortnights per month (instead of the 2.17 there are in real life), you will be surprised how quickly you get used to the new repayment schedule.

Until a few years ago, paying more each year by making the fortnightly payment 50 per cent of the monthly payment was the only way that paying fortnightly instead of monthly actually saved you money. This was because lenders used to calculate interest monthly based on the *month-end* mortgage balance. However, many lenders now calculate interest monthly on the *daily* balances *during* the month, so paying fortnightly can save you money, even if you don't pay more off per year.

If your lender calculates interest this way and if you make fortnightly payments of 46 per cent of the monthly amount, all you are doing is splitting 12 monthly payments into 26 fortnightly payments each year, so you pay no more each year than if you were making the correct monthly payment each month. But, because your average daily loan balance is now lower during each month, you save interest. The benefit is small — it saves $3000 in interest and knocks two months off the term — but that's a $3000 benefit without you paying a single cent more.

Of course, it is much better to go for the fortnightly payments of 50 per cent of the monthly amount if you can. That way you get it paid off much sooner and with very little difference to your day-to-day budgeting.

18 Shop around for a lower rate

Reducing the interest rate on your mortgage by even a small amount can save you a fortune in interest. Let's say you have a 25-year $300 000 mortgage currently at 7 per cent, with monthly repayments of $2120.34. If you can reduce the rate by 0.5 per cent and you reduce the repayments to the new lower level of $2025.62, it cuts your total interest bill by 8.5 per cent and saves you $28 000 in interest over the full term.

Table 3.7 helps estimate your savings if you reduce your interest rate and also reduce the monthly repayments.

Table 3.7: impact of interest rate reduction if repayments are reduced*

Term remaining	6.00% Interest saved	7.00% Interest saved	8.00% Interest saved	9.00% Interest saved	10.00% Interest saved
10 years	$602	$618	$633	$649	$664
15 years	$971	$1005	$1038	$1069	$1100
20 years	$1382	$1438	$1491	$1541	$1588
25 years	$1830	$1910	$1984	$2051	$2112
30 years	$2309	$2413	$2505	$2587	$2657

*Interest saving per 0.1 per cent interest rate reduction per $100 000 loan.

If you have a $250 000 mortgage at 8 per cent with 25 years to go, a rate reduction of 0.2 per cent reduces the repayments from $1930 per month to $1897. This results in a total interest saving of $1984 (from the above table) × 2.5 (for a $250 000 mortgage) × 2 (for 0.2 per cent rate reduction) = approx $9900.

The first place to start looking for a better interest rate deal is with your current lender. They are not going to recommend a lower rate mortgage to you if you don't ask them. They'll usually stitch you up for the highest rate they can get away with, so it's up to you to find the best deal for your circumstances.

Even after you have investigated the best rate basic loan your current lender has to offer, you can still look around to see what else is available in the market. There is always a range of lenders that tend to have very low rates consistently. Probably nine out of 10 borrowers will find that they can get a better rate on their mortgage if they shop around.

The general rule of thumb is: if the interest rate on your mortgage is 0.75 per cent to one per cent more than the current official cash rate, there are probably going to be better deals around. Lenders are free to set the interest rates on all their loans, but the pricing of variable rate mortgages is based on the short-term money market, which is based on the official cash target rate. This is set by the Reserve Bank of Australia and rises and falls as the economy grows and slows over each economic cycle. Mortgage rates rise and fall along with the official cash target rate. You can check the current cash rate on the Reserve Bank of Australia home page <www.rba.gov.au> listed under 'target cash rate'.

There are many websites where you can check out mortgage rates on hundreds of different loans from dozens of lenders. Try these:

- $ <www.yourmortgage.com.au>
- $ <www.infochoice.com.au>
- $ <www.cannex.com.au>
- $ <www.ratecity.com.au>.

There are also good magazines to help you research lenders:

- $ *Your Mortgage* is full of tables and comparisons of mortgages
- $ *Money* covers all personal finance topics, including mortgages
- $ *Smart Investor* often has articles and tables on mortgage and mortgage lenders.

Another approach is to use a mortgage broker. Use your existing mortgage broker if you have one, or ask friends and family for recommendations. Use competitors' rates as a bargaining chip to get your existing lender to match the competitor rate.

19 Keep repayments flat when rates fall

Whenever your mortgage interest rate falls, or after you've managed to reduce the interest rate through renegotiation or refinance, it saves you interest if you reduce the repayments to the new lower level with the lower interest rate. However, if you don't reduce the repayments you will save much more interest and get out of debt much sooner. This is a painless way to make big inroads into your mortgage.

Let's say you have a 25-year, $300000 mortgage currently at 7 per cent with monthly repayments at $2120.34. If the rate reduces by 0.5 per cent, but your repayments are kept at the old level, your total interest bill is cut by a massive 19 per cent. It saves you more than $65000 in interest and you pay off the whole loan 31 months sooner.

If you could afford the payments on the existing loan, then you can keep them at the same level once the interest rate is lower. You could reduce the repayments to the new lower level at 6.5 per cent, but that would put just $95 per month or $3 per day into your pocket. This is loose change and it would probably just get eaten up in day-to-day living expenses. So put this extra $3 per day to work and use it to get rid of the mortgage sooner by keeping the repayments at the old level instead.

Even reducing the interest rate by just 0.1 per cent and keeping the repayments at the same level, you can save $15000 in interest and pay off the loan seven months sooner.

Table 3.8 (overleaf) helps you estimate the interest savings and months saved by reducing the rate but not reducing the repayment amount.

Table 3.8: impact of rate reduction if repayments remain at same level*

Current interest rate	6.00%		7.00%		8.00%	
Term remaining	Interest saved	Months saved	Interest saved	Months saved	Interest saved	Months saved
10 years	$818	0.7	$887	0.8	$961	0.8
15 years	$1552	1.8	$1749	1.9	$1970	2.1
20 years	$2612	3.6	$3057	3.9	$3576	4.3
25 years	$4107	6.4	$4989	7.1	$6050	7.8
30 years	$6178	10.3	$7774	11.7	$9758	13.3

Current interest rate	9.00%		10.00%	
Term remaining	Interest saved	Months saved	Interest saved	Months saved
10 years	$1041	0.8	$1127	0.9
15 years	$2218	2.2	$2495	2.3
20 years	$4178	4.6	$4877	5.1
25 years	$7325	8.7	$8857	9.7
30 years	$12219	15.2	$15256	17.4

*Interest saved per 0.1 per cent rate reduction per $100 000 loan, and months saved per 0.1 per cent rate reduction.

For example, say you have a $250 000 mortgage at 8 per cent interest with 25 years left to pay the loan. If your interest rate is reduced by 0.2 per cent but you keep repayments at the old level instead of reducing them, it results in an interest saving of $6050 (from the table) × 2.5 (for a $250 000 mortgage) × 2 (for 0.2 per cent rate reduction) = approx $30 000. It also means you pay off the loan sooner by 7.8 months (from the table) × 2 (for 0.2 per cent rate reduction) = 15 months. This is a much better result than if you reduce the repayments when the rate is reduced.

20 Don't keep switching loans

When refinancing, it is important to focus on the long-term savings and avoid the temptation to constantly chase the lowest short-term rates in the market. If you repeatedly switch from loan to loan, chasing the best rate each year, the costs of financing tend to outweigh any savings. You also need to cost in all your time and effort, and all the headaches and hassles involved in constantly shopping around and switching.

I know some people who make it their life's mission to always chase the lowest mortgage rate in the market, but I find that 10 or even 20 years later they are still on the mortgage treadmill. They should have devoted all that energy to actually paying off the mortgage instead, so they'd never have to worry about it again!

Refinancing your mortgage is not without costs. Many lenders charge 'penalty interest' for early repayment. Often the penalties are higher if the loan is repaid in the first year or so of the mortgage. This is one of the key factors you should always find out about when taking out a mortgage.

The new lender usually wants to charge an application fee (maybe $500), plus a couple of hundred dollars each for legal fees and a valuation. In most states there is also mortgage stamp duty of several hundred dollars per $100000 borrowed. If you are refinancing with the same lender there will be no stamp duty (unless you are increasing the loan amount) and it should also not charge fees for application, legal or valuation. The lender will try, but tell it you'll just go to another lender if it does.

If you are refinancing with a new lender you will not be able to avoid the mortgage stamp duty, so make sure the savings in interest more than outweigh the extra cost. For example, mortgage stamp duty of 0.4 per cent on a $300 000 loan is $1200, plus other upfront fees of, say, $500 make the total $1700. If you are reducing the interest rate by 0.5 per cent, that's a saving of $1500 in interest each year. So the stamp duty is paid by the lower interest rate in a little over one year. Stamp duties in each state and territory differ, so check your local rules first.

Try to get the new lender to reduce or waive any upfront fees. Generally the larger the loan and the more business you can offer the lender (such as investment property loans or investment accounts), the more bargaining power you have. Lenders are under enormous pressure to make their monthly lending budgets so they are usually very eager to negotiate to get your business. If you ask for a discount and make it look like you are expecting to get one, nine times out of 10 it will work.

One of the great problems with shopping around to chase the lowest rate is that mortgage rates change every few months with the changes in the money market. Each time rates change, not all lenders change all their rates by the same amount. This means that a lender with the lowest rates one year will often not have the lowest rates next year. To always have the lowest rate you need to switch lenders every few months or every year and that will never be cost-effective.

If you have a plan to pay off the mortgage in, say, five years, focus your refinancing effort on finding a loan that has consistently been among the lowest rates over several years (but not necessarily the absolute lowest rate) instead of constantly switching from loan to loan. Then put all your efforts into paying off and getting rid of the mortgage forever.

21 When refinancing, stick with your existing lender if you can

When refinancing into a better loan, staying with your existing lender is almost always cheaper than shifting to a new lender. Your existing lender already has the mortgage documentation, title deeds and property valuation. You already have a credit history with them, so the costs of setting up a new loan are much lower than if you were a brand new customer to them and you are already a 'known quantity' so they will be keen to keep you on their books.

When you are negotiating with the lender to refinance your loan it is always better to have an alternative lined up with which you can ask them to compete. It is very powerful to be able to pull out a letter of offer from another lender to prove that you are serious about leaving them if they don't match the offer.

Large lenders have several divisions and departments that all compete with each other for deals. In most cases they will even undercut each other to win your business. This may seem strange to most people, but they figure that it is better to keep you in their group than let you leave altogether and go to another lender.

The sales reps at most lenders get paid sales commission, or are on a salary structure that varies based on how many new deals they bring in. Generally their sales commissions and salary structures even include deals they take from other departments of the same lender!

22 Always choose principal-and-interest loans over interest-only loans

Most home mortgages in Australia are principal-and-interest (P&I), which means that a portion of each repayment goes towards paying the principal balance so, by the end of the loan term, the balance is paid off completely. We have already seen with P&I loans how lengthening the term of the loan adds substantially to the total interest bill and slows the rate at which the loan balance reduces, so you stay in more debt for longer.

Interest-only loans are the ultimate in long-term loans. Unless you sell the house or switch into a P&I loan, you'll never get rid of the mortgage and you'll be paying interest forever.

Repayments on interest-only loans are lower than P&I loans because you're not repaying any principal off the balance. This sounds attractive in theory, but in practice this is generally not a good thing because it just encourages lenders to lend you more money and encourages borrowers to borrow more than they otherwise would.

Let's get back to basics. A home bought with borrowed money is not an investment, it is a savings plan. It is not an investment because even well-located residential property grows in value only by about 2 to 3 per cent above the inflation rate over the long term, but the interest rates on housing loans are also around 2 to 3 per cent above the inflation rate, so you don't build any real equity in your home unless you pay off the loan. A P&I mortgage is a good savings plan because it forces you to pay back part of the principal each month, so you build real equity over time. An interest-only loan is only a partial savings plan because you are only forced to cover the interest on the loan, but never actually pay off the loan itself.

If you currently have an interest-only mortgage on your home and want to get out of debt one day, you need to either sell and trade down to a cheaper home or get into a P&I mortgage. Assuming you want to stay in your home, that means shifting from interest-only to P&I.

Think back to when you took out the loan initially. Your income has probably risen since then, but for most people, extra income somehow just disappears in higher spending. You need to find where that extra money is going and start putting some of it towards paying off the principal with a P&I loan.

If you have a loan of $300 000 at 7 per cent, the interest-only repayments are $1750 per month. Switching into a 25-year P&I loan at the same interest rate means repayments jump by 21 per cent to $2120 per month. Switching to a 30-year P&I loan means repayments jump by 14 per cent to $1996 per month. This is a jump of $246 per month, or $8 per day. Start thinking where that $8 per day is currently going and make a plan to put it into the mortgage instead.

Most interest-only mortgages don't allow you to make principal reductions or additional repayments. P&I loans are generally more flexible, with fewer restrictions on making principal reductions and irregular or occasional extra repayments. It is also easier to renegotiate terms. Ring your lender and ask it what the rules are for your current mortgage. Usually you will need to renegotiate out of the interest-only loan into a new P&I loan with new mortgage documents. If you stay with your current lender you will minimise refinancing costs.

23 Stick with floating mortgages

Most mortgages in Australia are variable rate (also called floating rate) loans, meaning that the interest rate and repayments vary with interest rates in the overall economic cycle. In economic booms, when employment, incomes and inflation are rising, short-term interest rates in the general economy rise, taking variable mortgage rates up with them. Then, as the economy slows down, when employment, incomes and inflation fall, short-term interest rates and variable mortgage rates fall as well. As the interest rates on variable rate mortgages go up and down, so do the monthly repayments.

With fixed-rate mortgages the interest rate and loan repayments are set at a fixed level for the term of the loan, which is usually one, three or five years in Australia. (Some lenders offer terms up to 10 years, but interest rates are very expensive because the market for them is not large. This is very different from the US where most home mortgages are fixed for 30 years, with a provision allowing the borrower to reduce rates whenever fixed rates fall. This unique feature in the US mortgage market is one of the main reasons US mortgage lenders regularly get into trouble, including the late 1980s savings and loan collapses and the 2008 subprime crisis.)

The main advantage of fixed-rate loans is that the repayments are fixed and certain. But this 'certainty' lasts only for the one-, three- or five-year term of the fixed-rate loan. Then you need to refinance (or roll over) the loan into another fixed-rate loan or go to a variable rate. If rates have moved up over the period, then you will be hit with higher rates. You can't eliminate the risk.

This certainty of fixed-rate repayments is marketed as a good thing because people's incomes are also fixed and certain. But this is an illusion. Most people's incomes are neither fixed nor certain. During economic booms, incomes rise along with inflation, business revenues and profits rise, rental income rises, and personal incomes rise through pay increases, more overtime, extra shifts, bonuses and the availability of extra jobs, so there is generally more money coming in to pay the higher variable mortgage payments when mortgage interest rates rise. In economic recessions and slowdowns, incomes fall. Falling business revenues and profits, falling rental income, less overtime, reduced bonuses, fewer shifts and more job losses means there is less money coming in, but mortgage rates and repayments also fall during the slowdown part of the cycle.

Fixed-rate loans have two further disadvantages. The first is that people tend to lock into fixed-rate loans at the wrong time, when interest rates have been rising for a while and are nearing their peak. That's generally near the top of the economic cycle, immediately before rates fall. Thousands of people panicked and piled into fixed-rate mortgages when interest rates were high and rising strongly in 1988–89, 1994, 2000 and 2006–08, and they missed out on the interest rate falls in the slowdowns that followed. Many readers may recall when mortgage rates were up around 18 per cent in the late 1980s. I remember—I had one! The people who had locked into fixed rates were paying crippling repayments during the early 1990s recession when variable interest rates dropped by more than half. More recently, many thousands of borrowers panicked and locked in when rates were high in 2007 and early 2008 and kept paying through the nose as variable rates fell dramatically in the 2008–09 recession.

The second disadvantage of fixed-rate loans is that they generally don't allow borrowers to increase repayments or make extra repayments to reduce the principal faster. Nor do they allow you to pay out the loan early without heavy penalties, as you can with most variable rate loans. Paying out fixed-rate loans early when rates are falling can often cost tens of thousands of dollars in interest penalties.

Most lenders offer an option to split a loan into a fixed portion and a floating portion, and most also offer borrowers the option to alter the proportions. These options come at a cost, either in a higher interest rate or extra fees. Unfortunately, from my experience, if people are given such options, they tend to either fiddle with the proportions too frequently, panic and switch at the wrong time, or not use them at all, so these features are often a waste of money.

The bottom line is that most Australians are better off with a variable rate mortgage, rather than constantly trying to pick the best timing for fixed-rate periods. Stick with variable rates, then put all your energy into paying it off as quickly as possible so you don't have to worry about mortgage rates ever again.

24 Avoid redraw mortgages

The redraw mortgage was another 'innovation' of the 1990s that sounded great initially, but it was really just another trick lenders used to keep borrowers in debt for longer. These days just about every lender offers redraw options on their mortgages, always at a higher interest rate than their basic no-frills mortgage.

A mortgage with a redraw facility allows the borrower to redraw the principal they have paid off the balance. For example, if you started out with a $300 000 mortgage over 25 years at 7 per cent, after five years the balance will have reduced to $273 486, so $26 514 has come off the principal. A redraw facility allows the borrower to re-borrow this $26 514 so the mortgage goes back to the original $300 000. Paying off the mortgage once is hard enough. Why would you want to *repay* money you've already repaid once?

In the first five years of the loan, the borrower would have paid a massive $127 220 in total payments to the lender, but just 21 per cent of the payments reduce the balance. Nearly 80 per cent of the repayments pay interest to the lender. Reducing the balance is tough! Why would you want to start out all over again by redrawing it back to the original amount?

Don't be tempted to redraw money from the mortgage to pay for living expenses or depreciating assets such as cars, boats, furniture, holidays and renovations. The rule of thumb is if you can't pay cash for living expenses and depreciating items, then you can't afford them. Never borrow to buy depreciating assets.

As an example of how bad redraw mortgages are, let's say you start out with a $300 000 mortgage at seven per cent for 25 years. You redraw $15 000 at the end of year three to buy a car, and another $20 000 at the end of year seven to buy a boat, and keep making the same regular repayments. If you didn't redraw you would end up paying off the mortgage fully at the end of the 25-year term. But by making the two redraws you would still owe $139 000 at the end of 25 years! Unless you sold the house to clear the debt, you would need to refinance this balance and, if you kept the same repayments and same interest rate, it would keep you in debt for another seven years. Figure 3.6 (overleaf) shows how it would look.

The $15 000 car and $20 000 boat end up costing you a massive $139 000, and they keep you in debt for seven years longer! Don't do it!

If you use some or all of the money you redraw to purchase investments or business assets, you generally won't be able to claim a tax deduction on the interest because the loan is not a separate account, it is part of the original housing loan. It is much better to take out a separate low interest rate, no-frills loan for the business or investment asset and claim a tax deduction on the interest.

If you have a redraw facility on your mortgage, the best thing to do with it is to never use it. But the problem is that you're still paying for it every day in the form of higher interest rates charged on redraw loans. It is better to switch to a basic no-frills loan at a lower interest rate where you can't make redraws.

Figure 3.6: extra interest paid if the redraw mortgage is used

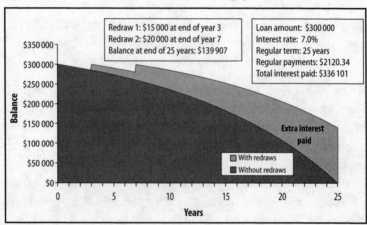

25 Be careful of offset accounts

A mortgage offset account is a deposit account linked to your mortgage account. When interest is calculated on your mortgage balance each month, if there is any money sitting in the offset account the mortgage interest is calculated on just the net amount; that is, the mortgage balance less the offset account balance.

If used wisely, offset accounts can be a great way to pay off the mortgage sooner. They allow you to use spare cash (for example, cash left over from your salary after everyday expenses are paid) to reduce the interest bill on your mortgage. This means more of your regular monthly mortgage payments go towards reducing the principal balance.

For example, if you have a 25-year, $300 000 mortgage at 7 per cent, the monthly repayments will be $2120.34. If you are, say, five years into the loan, the current balance will be $273 486. Out of your regular monthly repayment, $1595.34 of it is interest that goes to the bank and just $525 goes towards reducing your loan balance that month.

Let's say you had $10 000 cash sitting in an account (not an offset account) for a 31-day month earning interest of 5 per cent, so you earn interest income of $42.47 for the month. Interest on cash accounts is taxable, so you receive $29.09 after tax if you are in the 31.5 per cent income tax bracket (like most Australian workers). So, having $10 000 sitting in a separate cash account earning interest for a month makes you $29.09 better off after tax.

On the other hand, if you put that same $10 000 cash into a mortgage offset account linked to your mortgage, this account doesn't earn interest in the normal way, but is used to offset your mortgage balance for the purpose of calculating interest on the mortgage. Your mortgage interest for that month is calculated on the net $263 486 balance, not the full $273 486 mortgage balance, so your mortgage interest bill for the month is $59.45 lower, and this extra $59.45 goes towards reducing your mortgage balance.

You are $59.45 better off and you are not taxed on this benefit, so your net return (or net benefit to you after tax) is *double* what it would be if it were sitting in a separate cash account earning taxable interest.

Interest on most variable rate principal-and-interest mortgages is calculated on the daily net balance, so even small amounts of money in the offset account for a few days can really make a difference over time. One common approach is to have your entire salary paid straight into the offset account, then take money out during the month to pay living expenses. Every dollar sitting in the offset account reduces the interest bill on the mortgage account and puts the extra money into paying down the mortgage balance.

As cash builds up in your offset account from month to month, it can be tempting to spend it. Banks want you to do this because it keeps you in debt longer, but it is much better to use that extra cash to get rid of the mortgage and never have to pay it back to the bank again! If a surplus builds up in your offset account, transfer it across to the mortgage permanently so it's paid off forever.

If you had just $1000 sitting in your offset account for the whole period of the mortgage, it would reduce your total interest for the mortgage by nearly $5000 and pay off a typical 25-year $300 000 mortgage three months sooner.

Loans with offset facilities generally cost more than basic no-frills or 'vanilla' mortgages, so make sure you are making best use of it.

26 Don't use line-of-credit mortgages

A line-of-credit mortgage is another innovation that is a sure-fire way of keeping you in debt years longer than necessary. Let's say your house is worth $500 000 and your existing debt is $300 000. A lender will give you a line of credit with a credit limit of approximately $400 000 (they are usually limited to 80 per cent of the house value). The lender will then give you a cheque book so that you can write cheques to draw down to the credit limit, and a deposit book. It sounds great—another $100 000 to spend!

But beware! Line-of-credit mortgages are even worse than redraw mortgages because they often don't have a set repayment schedule, so there is no built-in mechanism to pay off the debt, unlike Principal-and-interest loans. Unless you have the discipline to pay enough off each month to at least cover the interest, the balance keeps building up (capitalising) and pretty soon you are up to the limit. It's a bit like a credit card except the amounts are much bigger so they can get you into trouble even faster.

Don't use your line of credit to pay for consumption expenses like everyday household expenses, holidays and weddings. Also, never use it for buying depreciating assets such as cars, boats, furniture and renovations. Lines of credit have lower interest rates than car loans, personal loans and other types of personal debt because they are secured by real estate, but the rates are still higher than for basic no-frills mortgages.

For most people, what starts out as temporary debt soon turns into long-term core debt that hangs around for years. Never let this happen. Only use lines of credit for short-term cash needs where you have a specific plan of action to clear the debt. For example, it is generally not a good idea to pay for home renovations using a mortgage or line of credit because the renovations almost always depreciate quickly, but you can be paying for the renovations for the next 25 years. It would make sense to do this only if you intend to sell the house as soon as the renovations are complete, so that the renovations are still new and in fashion.

These days most banks offer ATM and EFTPOS access to credit accounts. This sounds very convenient but is extremely dangerous! For most people the temptation to use credit for everyday expenses is too great. Pretty soon the line of credit is up to the limit and they end up paying for groceries for the next 30 years!

Lines of credit can also be linked to other accounts via internet banking. This, too, sounds convenient, but it is dangerous. Most people start out with the intention of using the online access to pay off the line of credit with spare cash sitting in their transaction account, but usually this never happens. It is just too tempting to shift money the other way—out of the line of credit and into the transaction account—with just a click of a mouse.

The best plan for paying off a line of credit is to set up an automatic credit from your transaction account or, better still, your salary, so it happens without you having to do it manually.

Cheque book access is useful for making payments that you genuinely should use a line of credit for, but this, too, is a temptation that should be avoided. If the cheque book is sitting in the drawer next to your other cheque books, it is too easy to reach for it to pay regular bills like electricity, water and gas. The best plan is to have no cheque book access either. When you need to pay an amount using the line of credit, have the bank prepare a bank cheque. If the bank charges a fee of $10 or so for bank cheques this will be a small price to pay compared with the consequences of using the line of credit to pay regular household expenses.

27 Beware the honeymoon rate nightmare

Most lenders offer products with a low interest rate for a short introductory or honeymoon period at the start of the loan (usually between six months and three years), after which it reverts to a higher interest rate for the rest of the period of 25 or 30 years.

Their 'normal' interest rate for the remaining period is always higher than their regular rate on their basic no-frills loans, so you end up paying 1 per cent or so lower during the honeymoon period, then a 0.5 per cent or 1 per cent higher rate for the rest of the loan term. This type of loan is also sometimes called a 'step-up loan'.

This is a marketing trick aimed primarily at first home buyers to get them to borrow more than they should, because the initial repayments are artificially low. There are always heavy penalties and fees to discourage refinancing after the initial low rate period, because the lenders want to lock you in for as long as possible.

There are two main types of honeymoon loans and the difference between them is in what happens during the initial period. The first type has a fixed-rate, interest-only loan during the initial period, followed by a higher variable rate principal-and-interest loan for the remaining period. We will look at this type first as it's the most common.

For example, for a standard 25-year principal-and-interest loan for $300 000 at 7 per cent the repayments are $2120.34 per month. Total interest paid over the whole period is $336 101 plus the repayment of the $300 000 originally borrowed.

A popular honeymoon deal is a three-year, fixed-rate interest-only honeymoon period followed by a 22-year principal-and-interest loan, making a total of 25 years. If the three-year, fixed-rate interest-only period is at 5 per cent and the 22-year principal-and-interest period is at 7.5 per cent, the repayment schedule is:

$ 36 monthly payments of $1250, followed by

$ 264 monthly payments of $2323.53.

With these types of loans, the loan is interest-only for the initial period, so you make only the interest payments (in this example at the rate of 5 per cent). The principal balance remains constant at the initial $300 000 borrowed and doesn't start reducing until the principal-and-interest stage commences in month 37.

This honeymoon deal ends up costing you $22 311 more in interest over the whole period, compared with a standard 25-year P&I loan at 7 per cent. Not only is the interest bill higher, but the loan starts reducing later and, when it does start reducing, it reduces more slowly than the standard 25-year loan, so you owe more at any given stage during the loan if you decide to pay out the loan early (such as when you sell the house). For example, after 10 years into the deal, the loan balance is $14 740 higher with the honeymoon deal compared with the standard 25-year loan. Figure 3.7 shows the balance over the loan period.

Figure 3.7: fixed rate honeymoon mortgage

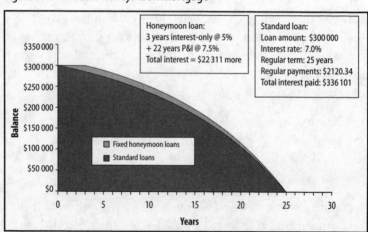

28 Don't capitalise loans

A second type of honeymoon deal also has lower repayments during the initial honeymoon period and higher payments during the remaining period, but the same interest rate applies to the whole period. Because the higher interest rate applies even to the initial period, the lower repayments don't cover the interest on the loan and the shortfall is added to the loan so the loan balance *grows* (or capitalises) rather than staying constant or reducing. They are often called capitalising loans. At the end of the honeymoon period, the loan converts to principal-and-interest based on the new *higher* balance and the same interest rate, so the repayments are much higher for the remaining years.

For example, a $300 000 loan might have an interest rate for the whole period of 7.5 per cent, but have repayments calculated at 5 per cent of the amount borrowed ($1250 per month) for the first 36 months. Because the loan balance is still being calculated at the set rate of 7.5 per cent, the balance creeps up each month because your repayments don't fully cover the interest bill. The shortfall is added to the loan each month, so by the end of the third year the balance has blown out to $325 145, but then starts to reduce slowly over the remaining 22 years. Figure 3.8 illustrates how the balance looks over time compared with a standard 25-year loan.

Figure 3.8: capitalising honeymoon mortgage

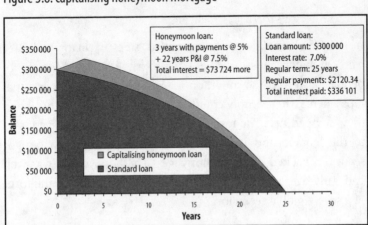

The total interest payable is a hefty $73 724 more than a standard 25-year loan at 7 per cent. If you sell the house and pay out the loan at the end of 10 years, the balance is a whopping $35 750 higher with this honeymoon deal compared with the standard 25-year loan. Some honeymoon!

All honeymoon deals are dangerous because they lure borrowers into a false sense of what they can afford on their income. They trap young borrowers into mortgages that aren't reducing (or even worse, are growing) over the first few years. Reality hits when the honeymoon period ends and the repayments jump to the higher level. In most cases, the borrowers haven't saved the difference between the low honeymoon rates and what the regular payments would have been with a standard loan. Instead they have simply borrowed more to buy a more expensive house or they have spent the difference.

If you have one of these loans, find out *today* what the higher payments will be and exactly what date they start. Start planning how you will pay this higher amount and put the extra cash away in an account so you have an emergency fund ready for when the repayments jump.

In the US, loans like these are called 'step-up' loans and they were a major cause of the US subprime crisis. Millions of people borrowed too much on loans with artificially low initial repayments, then simply couldn't pay the higher payments when they 'stepped up'. The resulting bad debts caused massive losses to the lenders and investors all over the world who bought securities backed by these mortgages. The honeymoon was well and truly over and it resulted in a massive hangover in the form of a severe global recession.

29 Upgrade your subprime loan

Subprime or non-conforming loans are loans made to people with poor credit ratings or who lack documentation to verify their income or assets. Often the poor credit rating or lack of documentation is not the fault of the borrower. It may be due to a divorce or failure of a partner's business. Another common reason is that new immigrants either have difficulty in verifying past income in their old country, or because they haven't had time to build up a credit history in their new country.

These types of loans are called different things by different lenders, but just about all lenders these days offer them. Some are called low-doc or no-doc loans, referring to the lack of documentation needed to support the borrower's ability to make the repayments or verify assets. Others are called credit-impaired loans, referring to the poor credit history of the borrower.

Non-conforming or subprime loans generally have interest rates 2 to 5 per cent higher than conforming or prime loans. The higher interest rate is to compensate the lender for the higher risk of default and loss.

Although subprime mortgages have recently developed a bad name due to the massive problems in the US market, there is nothing wrong with having one if you use it the right way. Often they are the only means available for some borrowers to get into the housing market.

If you have one of these mortgages and have been making your repayments on time for a few years, you will have significantly improved your credit rating. You probably now qualify for a lower interest rate, 'prime' mortgage. If yours is a low-doc or no-doc loan you will also have had a few years to build up documentation of your income and this will provide evidence of your ability to make regular loan repayments, together with the fact that you have been making repayments on time.

Go back to your current lender and ask if you can switch to a prime or conforming loan. Also, make applications to other lenders and see if you can refinance into a lower rate regular prime (or standard) mortgage.

Keep the repayments at the current level and you will pay off the mortgage quickly, saving several years in the process. For example, if five years ago you started a 25-year, $300 000 mortgage at 10 per cent, the repayments would be $2726 per month and the current balance would be $282 491. If you refinanced into a prime mortgage at 7 per cent with the same level of repayments as the old 10 per cent mortgage, you would pay off the loan in a little over 13 years, saving you nearly seven years and $218 000 in interest. By doing this you pay less interest and get out of debt sooner than a regular 'prime' borrower who took out a 25-year loan at 7 per cent. That's a great result from a rocky start!

30 Consolidate debt at your peril!

Most mortgage brokers like debt consolidation loans because it means you take out a bigger mortgage and this means bigger sales commissions. Let's say you have the loans shown in table 3.9.

A consolidation loan would add all the high-rate debts into the mortgage, which would increase to $350 000 and clear the other debts. It sounds good — you have no more high interest rate loans, just a bigger mortgage at the low rate. But this is a trap. You end up paying for the car, holiday and credit card over 25 years, and it will end up costing you a lot more money in the long run.

Table 3.9: consolidation loans — before consolidation

Type	Amount	Term (years)	Rate	Monthly repayments	Total payments	Total interest
Mortgage	$300 000	25	7%	$2120.34	$636 101	$336 101
Car loan	$30 000	5	12%	$667.33	$40 040	$10 040
Personal loan (for holiday)	$10 000	5	15%	$237.90	$14 274	$4 274
Credit cards	$10 000	—	15%	$500 (5% of balance)	$13 333	$3 333
Total	$350 000			$3525.57	$703 749	$353 749

For example, let's take the $30 000 car loan at 12 per cent payable over five years. If you refinance it by increasing your home loan by $30 000 you can reduce the interest rate from the original 12 per cent car loan rate to the home loan rate of 7 per cent per year. The payments on the car are reduced from the old $667.33 per month to $212.03 per month in the mortgage, so you are $455.30 per month better off. But, because you are now paying for the car over 25 years, the total cash outlay is $212.03 × 300 months = $63 609. You end up paying $33 609 in interest for the car, which is more than three times the interest you would have paid with the original car loan.

If you buy a new car every, say, seven years using your 25-year mortgage each time, then in 25 years' time you'll be up to your fourth car but you will still be paying off all four cars, even though the first three cars are long gone!

Table 3.10 (overleaf) illustrates what the full consolidation loan looks like.

Table 3.10: consolidation loan after consolidating into bigger mortgage

Type	Amount	Term (years)	Rate	Monthly repayments	Total payments	Total interest
Consolidation mortgage	$350 000	25	7%	$2473.73	$742 118	$392 118

The high-rate loans are now at a lower rate, but it ends up costing you $38 270 more in total interest.

Instead of consolidating high-rate debts into your mortgage, keep the existing mortgage as it is and consolidate the high-rate loans into a separate mortgage loan, secured by the same house at the same 7 per cent rate, but with a much shorter period. (These used to be called second mortgages and were at a higher rate, but these days you can take out several mortgages at the same home loan rate, as long as you have equity in your house.)

Since you are currently paying $1405.34 in monthly payments for the high-rate loans, make this the monthly repayment on the new loan, so you pay the whole lot off in a little over three years. Table 3.11 shows what the loans look like after being consolidated.

Table 3.11: consolidation loans after consolidating into a separate loan

Type	Amount	Term (years)	Rate	Monthly repayments	Total payments	Total interest
Existing mortgage	$300 000	25	7%	$2120.34	$636 101	$336 101
New second loan	$50 000	3.3	7%	$1405.23	$56 204	$6204
Total	$350 000			$3525.57	$692 306	$342 306

By doing this you pay $11 443 less interest than you are paying now and you get rid of the high-rate debts in just 40 months.

Perhaps the most dangerous aspect of consolidating high-rate debts like credit cards into your mortgage is that you end up with the same credit card in your wallet but no debt outstanding on it after you have transferred it to your mortgage. This means you have the full credit limit to spend all over again: 'Hey look, another $10000 to spend!' You may soon find yourself back up to the credit limit again and another $10000 in debt!

31 Don't pay for features you don't need

These days there are dozens of features and options attached to most mortgages, and new features are being invented all the time. They all add to the cost of the mortgage and most are simply designed to maximise revenue to the lender and keep you in debt for longer. The trick is to figure out which features are actually worth the extra money and which are not.

The bottom line is that a mortgage is a necessary evil. You should keep the interest rate as low as possible and pay it off as quickly as possible. Make sure you are not paying for any fancy extras you don't need.

Lenders use an old used-car-sales trick called 'bait and switch'. They advertise their lowest rate honeymoon loan or no-frills basic loan to get you in the door, then they up-sell you to a more expensive loan packed with features you don't need and fees you don't need to pay.

Some features can be useful in paying off the loan more quickly, including the following:

$ the ability to make additional one-off payments without attracting any fees

$ the ability to make one-off lump sum principal reductions with no fees

$ the ability to pay out the loan early with minimal fees

$ offset accounts with 100 per cent interest offset, calculated on daily balances

$ salary crediting direct to your mortgage

$ ability to make different payment frequencies—monthly, fortnightly or weekly.

None of these features costs any more to the lender, so don't pay any fees for them (see page 79 for tips on how to have fees reduced or waived).

Some features cost more and can be dangerous, including the following:

$ a redraw facility

$ the ability to switch between fixed and floating interest rates. Most people panic when interest rates change and switch the wrong way at the wrong time.

$ the ability to split the loan into fixed and floating portions

$ paper statements—some lenders charge you to send these

$ professional packages. They usually have slightly lower interest rates (up to 0.5 per cent lower), but there is often an annual fee, justified by a whole list of extra features that most people don't need. Don't pay for any such packages. Just ask for the lower rate and you will usually get it. Stick to a basic no-frills loan.

$ lines of credit—only use these for business purposes (see page 164)

$ the ability to reduce or skip payments for specified periods

$ 'portability'—a gimmick designed to keep you in debt as you change houses over the years

$ the ability to capitalise interest

$ an interest-only option, or the ability to switch to this option

$ card access to your mortgage via ATMs and EFTPOS

$ internet access to your mortgage

$ phone banking access to your mortgage.

All these extra means of accessing your mortgage are fine in theory. You can make extra payments to the mortgage from anywhere, anytime, 24/7, but in practice this never happens. What inevitably happens is that you end up taking money out of the mortgage 24/7 and you end up in more debt for longer.

32 Take into account all fees

When comparing different mortgages, you need to take into account not just the interest rate, but also the cost of all the fees and charges along the way. Lenders add all sorts of fees and charges to the loan in order to generate extra revenue. One loan with a 7 per cent rate might actually be cheaper than another loan at 6.75 per cent with a whole load of extra fees attached.

Upfront fees include all fees incurred at the start of the loan. Most lenders charge an application fee of at least a few hundred dollars. Many even try to charge an approval fee on top. There are also at least a few hundred dollars for the lender's valuation and legal costs, which are passed on to you. There are often all sorts of other fees, such as settlement fees and processing fees, but these are just revenue raisers because almost all the process is automated. Upfront fees range from about $500 to several thousand dollars for different lenders.

Many loans have monthly or annual fees. Again, these are pure revenue raisers as the process is automated and the lender's administrative costs are minimal.

Most loans are paid out early and most lenders charge payout fees as well. These can range from a couple of hundred dollars to several thousand dollars or several months interest. All fees should be set out in the letter of offer and documentation you receive at the start of the loan.

Let's compare two loans (see table 3.12). Both are for $300000, principal-and-interest loans over 25 years and both are paid out after seven years, which is the average life of mortgages in Australia.

Table 3.12: comparing mortgages with different fees

	Loan A (basic loan)	Loan B (low rate, high fees)
Interest rate	7.0%	6.75%
Monthly repayments	$2120.34	$2072.73
Total upfront fees	$500	$2000
Annual fee	Nil	$120
Payout fees	$500	3 months interest
Total interest and fees paid over life of loan	$139112	$140096
Actual effective annual rate including fees	7.05%	7.09%

Even though loan B is marketed as having a significantly lower rate than loan A and has lower monthly repayments, loan B ends up costing more over the seven-year average life of the loan. Low rate, high fee loans also tend to have other fees such as for making one-off extra payments, principal reductions and renegotiations.

You can find out the true rate of any loan using a simple spreadsheet in a few minutes. Personally, I would never trust a lender's calculations because they all use different formulas and assumptions. By all means try out the lender's online calculators, but always check the numbers yourself—you will be amazed at what tricks you find them using. Or you can ask an independent mortgage broker to do it for you. Most honest brokers will be happy to do it for you as part of their service. Ask a lot of questions and make sure they explain it in terms you understand.

33   *All fees are negotiable*

Lenders and mortgage brokers are amazed when borrowers take the list of fees at face value and don't negotiate them down. It's all a game—the more fees they get away with, the more the lender makes in profits, and the more the sales reps and brokers get in commissions. Nobody should ever pay the full fees asked—they are all negotiable. Most of the processes involved in consumer home mortgage lending are highly automated and there is very little human involvement anymore, so the costs are minimal.

Even fees paid by the lender to third parties, such as valuation fees and legal fees are highly negotiable. External valuers and law firms operate on very low bulk-fee discounts, but lenders often oncharge the borrower more for the services so they make a profit there too. They are using the third-party services as an excuse to extract more profits from you. Often the valuers don't even do proper valuations and the 'legals' are done by conveyancing firms instead of qualified lawyers, but the lender will still try to charge you high fees.

The valuation and legal work protects and benefits the lender, not you, so why should you pay for them? The lender is making hundreds of thousands of dollars in interest from you, so it should pay for its own legal work and valuations out of its cut. I have used this argument over the years and I nearly always get the fees reduced or waived.

Many lenders charge ongoing fees, either monthly or annually. There is no excuse for these fees since the payment process is completely automated these days. If lenders say they need the monthly or annual fee as part of their overall revenue, they are just admitting to being dishonest about the interest rate.

Payout fees are another huge cost to borrowers, because most loans are paid out early and very few actually last the full term of 25 or 30 years. A couple of hundred dollars for preparing and lodging the discharge of mortgage is all you should pay. Any additional fee, like a number of months interest, or a number of months repayments is purely a revenue-raising exercise by the lender. If you plan to pay out the mortgage early (as you should), make sure the payout fees are minimal.

Fees for one-off events, such as making additional repayments or lump sum principal reductions, should always be negotiated away. You need to be able to make extra payments and lump sums with no fees as part of your plan to get rid of the mortgage as quickly as possible.

Every borrower can get fees reduced or waived just by asking. Use the fee savings to borrow less money or put it into the mortgage and you will be out of debt sooner.

34 Don't count on your partner's income to borrow more

Before the lending boom of the 1990s and 2000s, most lenders didn't take into account a second income in the family when calculating repayments on a long-term mortgage. A second income was seen as a margin of safety, not a way for borrowers to borrow more money. It was a way borrowers could cover the mortgage payments if interest rates rose significantly or if the primary breadwinner's income fell. It was also a way of reducing the principal faster so the lender had more security cover and less risk, because recessions occurred every few years in which house prices — and lenders' security margins — suffered.

Things changed in the period between 1993 and 2008. In this 17-year-long boom with low interest rates, low inflation and no recessions, lenders forgot basic lending principles and they started to use a second income in the household to support bigger and bigger mortgages.

Not only did lenders count the second income in calculating how much people could borrow, but they also gave it *additional* weight in the calculations. This meant that if the family income doubles with the addition of the second income, the lenders' formulas allow you to borrow *more* than double the loan amount. For example, a single-income family earning $1000 per week after tax (about $60 000 per year gross) can borrow about $300 000 according to many lenders' formulas. However, if both partners bring in the same income each, the family would have a double income totaling $2000 per week and this would support borrowings of up to $700 000 according to the lenders' formulas, which is more than double the level for a single income. These amounts are ridiculous and I would never suggest people should have this much debt on those income levels, but it shows how silly the lenders' formulas are.

It makes no sense at all because in a high proportion of cases, the second income is largely eaten up in additional expenses that come with earning the second income such as transport, clothing, child care, babysitting, lunches and takeaway meals. You pay income tax on the extra income, but you don't get a deduction for the extra expenses involved in earning the extra income, so often you are no better off after tax.

If your family has a second income—before kids come along or after they are in school, or even if you plan to never have kids—use the extra money to make extra payments on the mortgage to pay it off sooner, so you can then focus on building wealth. Don't use it to borrow more money against the house or trade up to a more expensive house.

35 Mortgage brokers—spot the double take

Mortgage brokers are paid sales commissions from lenders to sell their loans for them. They get an upfront commission of about 0.7 per cent to 1 per cent of the loan amount when the loan is settled, and they also get an annual trailing commission of about 0.3 per cent of the outstanding balance per year. For a typical $300 000 loan they get paid about $2100 to $3000 upfront from the lender and then about $900 per year (reducing as your loan balance slowly reduces).

So if you have a $300 000 mortgage for, say, 10 years, the mortgage broker who sold you the loan will pocket around $6000 to $10 000 in sales commissions. Not bad for a few hours work! These commissions are paid by the lender out of the interest and fees you pay to the lender. The commissions are not added on top of your repayments. Of course, you are still paying for them indirectly because the cost of the sales commissions is built into the interest rate and fees you pay to the lender.

Unfortunately you can't go direct to the lender and expect to get a cheaper loan just because the lender doesn't have to pay the mortgage broker. Banks and other mortgage lenders sell most of their mortgages via mortgage brokers because paying the $10 000 commission to a mortgage broker is still cheaper than the cost of running a branch network. Branches are expensive and mortgage brokers are expensive—you end up paying for them either way.

These sales commission figures are for standard loans where the broker hasn't loaded an extra margin on top of the lender's normal interest rate. If the broker is able to load an extra, say, 0.5 per cent to the interest rate and/or an extra $500 to the upfront fees, the broker will pocket at least half of this as well as their normal commissions. If you haven't done your own homework to see what is available in the market, the broker will sense this quickly and will stitch you up with the highest interest rate and fees he or she can get away with. The higher the interest rate and fees, the more he or she pockets. The broker will make up all sorts of stories about why you don't qualify for a lower rate or lower fees.

Everybody who uses a mortgage broker should ring the lender direct as soon as they receive their approval to check that they are getting the best deal for their circumstances and to see if the broker is adding an extra margin to the interest rate and/or extra fees. The enquiry staff at lenders' call centres are generally on the side of customers and they are usually very helpful in identifying where brokers are trying to get more then they should. If they get you out of the broker's higher rate loan and put you back onto a regular loan, the broker will still get their normal commission, but they won't get away with any extra margin they load on top. If you save 0.5 per cent interest rate, it can save you $30 000 interest over the life of the loan.

If you are already in a loan obtained through a mortgage broker, you should still ring the lender's call centre to check if you are paying an extra margin that is going to the broker. Often you can switch into a regular loan at the lender's normal rate. Again, the broker will still get his or her normal commission, but will stop getting the extra margin. The sooner you stop paying extra margin, the less interest you pay and the faster you pay out the loan.

Many mortgage brokers also try to get a fee directly from borrowers on top of fees you pay to the lender. This is very common with non-English-speaking borrowers. *Never*, ever pay a fee direct to the mortgage broker. They are illegal in most states of Australia, but there are all sorts of ways brokers try to get around the rules. Your mortgage broker is already being paid by your lender, so there is no reason to pay twice. If the broker attempts to charge you a fee, ring the lender direct and ask for the sales manager. The manager should discipline the broker and in some cases will cut off their relationship with the broker.

36 Check that you are getting the correct rate changes

It always pays to check on the interest rates and loan repayments each time there is a change in rates. After your lender announces a rate change in the media, you will receive a letter setting out the new rate. Keep this and check that the repayments have actually changed by the right amount when you get the next statement. This may sound like overkill, but you would be surprised what tricks lenders regularly get up to.

For example, for many years I had two mortgages with the same bank on two investment properties on Queensland's Sunshine Coast. I had taken the mortgages out at different times and the loan codes on the bank's system were slightly different. Each bank has dozens of different loan codes on their system. There is virtually no such thing as a standard variable mortgage any more because there are so many combinations and permutations of different features. When the bank announces that it will reduce rates by, say, 0.25 per cent on its standard variable rate mortgages, don't assume that all of the different types of mortgages will get the full benefit of the 0.25 per cent rate cut.

In the case of the Sunshine Coast houses, because the two mortgages had different loan codes, the interest rates were always slightly different. One would always be about 0.08 per cent higher than the other, but nobody at the bank could explain why or make the rates the same. On numerous occasions when there was a general interest rate change, the rates on these two mortgages changed by different amounts. I had to ring up several times over the space of many years to get the bank to change the rates by the correct amount. On a couple of occasions, my rates did not change by the amount the bank announced on its standard variable rate loans, until I rang up and got the bank to do it.

As you would expect, all of the errors were in the bank's favour! Banks are very quick to pass on interest rate rises, but very slow to pass on rate cuts and sometimes only when you catch them out. Nobody is going to look after your interests except you.

37 Let a tenant pay the mortgage

Instead of battling on with a mortgage you can't afford, get a tenant to help you out. There are at least three main ways you can do this.

The first is to put a tenant into your house and move back home with your parents or grandparents for a few years. It can save you big money in child care, babysitting and coaching tuition for your kids. It can also save your parents or grandparents money, such as by not having to pay a handyperson do odd jobs around the house. There can be enormous psychological benefits on both sides from having more contact with family.

A second way is to move into a smaller house and put a tenant into yours, so the rent from the tenant covers all or part of your mortgage payments. The rent you receive will be taxable income, but you can generally claim a tax deduction for the interest you pay on your home loan while it is rented out, so it can be tax effective. The rent you pay on the house where you are staying is not tax deductible, but neither were the mortgage payments you were making when you were living at home.

If you sell your house after renting it out for up to six years, you can still get the owner-occupier exemption from capital gains tax on the sale. This can be a great result that can help pay off the debt while you pay no capital gains tax and have a tenant to help with the mortgage payments.

A third way to have tenants help pay the mortgage is to rent out one room or take in a boarder. In most cities there are thousands of backpackers, short-term workers, students, nurses and others who are looking for low-cost accommodation. Most houses in Australia have at least one extra room. The number of people per household has been falling steadily for a century but houses keep getting bigger, with more bedrooms. If the money gets tight, a large proportion of households in Australia could find a way to free up a spare room and turn it into extra income.

38 Consider long-term house-sitting

One of my readers contacted me a few years ago with an idea, which I have since seen applied successfully by several people.

Many people use house-sitters to look after their house for short periods while on holidays. Now simply take this idea one step further. Large firms of lawyers, accountants, management consultants, engineers and other types of professionals often have people going overseas regularly to work on projects lasting from a few months to a year or so. While the owner is away, having a house-sitter look after the house is often considered a better option than renting it out to tenants because house-sitters can do things most tenants won't, including looking after the garden, forwarding mail, doing minor repairs and maintenance and even looking after pets. It also means that the owner doesn't need to put their furniture into storage. A good house-sitter can string together several years of house-sitting for a number of houses, often from word of mouth referrals within the same firm of professionals.

Depending on the level of responsibilities agreed between owner and house-sitter, some arrangements involve the house-sitter paying a very low rent, other times no money changes hands and sometimes the owner pays the house-sitter a small amount.

If this type of lifestyle appeals to you, you can rent out your current house for a full market rent and claim the interest on your mortgage against the rental income. Because the rent you pay on the houses you house-sit will be minimal or nil, you will have much more cash that you can then use to pay off the mortgage, clear other debts and then accelerate your superannuation contributions and your investment plans.

There are a number of situations where long-term house-sitting can work well, including for divorced people, empty nesters and people trying to start over after a bad experience with debts. Most house-sitters tend to be singles or couples with no children, but I even know of families with young children who have done it for several years.

39 Plan a mortgage-burning party in advance

Paying off your mortgage is one of the great achievements of your adult life. When you finally make that last payment you get a tremendous feeling of relief, like an enormous weight has been lifted off your shoulders. It may not be a huge rush like your team winning the grand final—there is a bigger lead up with the mortgage because you know it's coming for a couple of years. But afterwards, the effect lasts much longer. After that last payment is made, you wake up every morning for several months with a sense of satisfaction and freedom that is hard to describe.

While you had the mortgage you worked the first two days of each week for the tax man, the next two days to pay the mortgage and only one day for yourself. Now, with the mortgage gone, you have an extra two days each week to work for yourself. You can choose to work less, or you can put the money into investments for later on, so you can retire sooner and live a better lifestyle.

Why not celebrate this new-found freedom with your friends and family? Using your debt-reduction plan, mark the date when you will make the last payment. By inviting people to a party to celebrate the event you are committing yourself to really stick to the plan. Once your friends and family know about it there is no turning back. It will keep you focused and on track for the target. Make it a separate event from a birthday or Christmas.

These days you don't actually get a mortgage back from the bank that you can burn, but you do get a discharge of mortgage document. You can't destroy this, because it must be lodged with the land titles office to take the mortgage off the title, so don't burn it in all the excitement!

40 Pay off the mortgage before investing

One of the most common debates I have with people is about how they can best use their spare cash. Is it better to pay off the mortgage, invest using their superannuation fund or invest outside the superannuation system?

Let's get one matter cleared up first: investing outside the superannuation system versus investing using superannuation. Superannuation is not an investment or investment class, it is just a legal structure through which you can invest. There are tax breaks available in the superannuation system, but in many cases the tax breaks are more than eaten up by massive fees charged by planners and superannuation fund managers. Generally, after taxes and fees are taken into account, if you want to invest in a particular asset you will be better off buying it through your superannuation fund instead of buying the same asset directly. This only applies if *all* of the following conditions are met:

$ you are not going to need the money until after you reach age 55 if you were born before 1 July 1960, or after you reach age 60 if you were born on or after 1 July 1964

$ you are in the 30 per cent tax bracket or higher

$ the contributions to superannuation are tax deductible because you are self-employed, a small business owner, or from your employer through salary sacrificing

$ you have your own self-managed superannuation fund

$ you keep the costs low by not paying for any platform fees, administration fees or managed fund fees.

Next, let's look at the choice between investing (whether via your superannuation fund or outside the superannuation system) versus paying off the mortgage. When considering any investment, including paying off the mortgage, there are three main factors to consider: return, risk and time period (often called time *horizon*). We will look at the *return* aspect first because that's all that most people and most advisers consider.

The major asset classes used for building long-term wealth are shares and property. This is because they generate capital growth income, they are tax effective and they have built-in hedges (or protection) against inflation. If you invest your surplus money in either shares or property, whether via your superannuation fund or outside the superannuation system, your return after taxes and fees over the long term will generally beat paying off the mortgage. Mortgage interest on your own home is not tax deductible and there are no management fees, so if you put your spare cash into paying off the mortgage, the return after taxes and fees is the same as the mortgage interest rate at the time you make the payment, which may be 7 per cent, for example.

On the other hand, if you put your spare cash into investments such as shares or property, your return *before* taxes and fees will average around 10 per cent to 12 per cent over the long term (or about 6 to 8 per cent above the inflation rate) if your shares or properties are well diversified. Because shares and property have significant tax breaks for long-term investors, your return *after* taxes and fees from shares and property will generally be only a couple of per cent lower than the return *before* taxes and fees. This is the case whether you do it inside your superannuation fund or outside the superannuation system. So, if you considered just the return aspect of the equation, investing in long-term growth assets will often beat paying off the mortgage.

The second aspect is *risk*, which is just as important as return. If you invest your spare cash in shares or property, whether via your superannuation account or outside superannuation, the value of your investments will never remain constant, they will vary up and down over time. If you invest $1000 today it might be worth a lot more or a lot less tomorrow, next year or in 10 years. Some years are tremendous years for shares and property, other years are disasters, such as 2008.

The problem is that most first-time investors buy in during the boom periods near the top of the market and are badly burned in the crashes that always follow the booms. Many thousands of people in Australia and many other countries invested in the sharemarket and commercial property market in the boom period between 2004 and 2007. Even worse, many thousands borrowed to invest near the top of the market and were financially ruined by the crash in both the sharemarkets and commercial property market in 2008.

On the other hand, paying off the mortgage has *no risk*. Every $1000 you pay off the mortgage reduces your debt and increases your net wealth by exactly $1000. You never lose this $1000 in increased net wealth—it is yours forever. Even 'safe' investments such as cash and government bonds have risk because their returns and values vary over time. Also the income from cash and bonds is taxable and they have no hedges against inflation.

The bottom line is this: you must always consider reward and risk together. On the basis of risk-adjusted returns after taxes, fees and inflation, *nothing* beats paying off the mortgage, not even growth assets such as shares or property and not even 'safe' investments such as cash or government bonds.

The third aspect to consider is your *time* period; that is, how soon you want your money back from your investments. If you put your $1000 into your mortgage, your net wealth increases by $1000 today and you will keep this increased wealth forever. If you invest in any assets via your superannuation fund, you will need to wait until you reach age 60 (or 55 if you were born before 1 July 1960) to get your hands on it. For investments outside the superannuation system, if you invest in shares or property, you generally need to allow at least five to 10 years to count on any growth in value. If you need the cash before then, there is a significant probability of losses.

There are some further advantages of paying off the mortgage.

$ A mortgage is a forced savings plan. You can't simply skip a month here and there if you feel like it, as you can with an investment plan. It is often extremely difficult to stick to an investment plan in practice — it requires superb determination and discipline. It is too easy for most people to simply spend surplus cash on day-to-day living expenses instead.

$ It is very tempting to blow your investments on a car, boat or holiday.

$ Nothing beats the sense of freedom, control, peace of mind and complete flexibility of having no debts.

The golden rule is (and always has been) to get out of debt first. Then you will have much more cash to invest and start to build wealth seriously.

If paying off the mortgage first is so much better than investing, why do so few people do it? The main reason is that there are too many distractions and too many so-called experts out there trying to make money from you. Experts don't like you paying off the mortgage because there's nothing in it for them. Financial planners get rich selling you their investment plans or superannuation schemes, fund managers get rich selling you their managed funds, stockbrokers get rich selling you shares, real estate agents get rich selling you property, finance brokers get rich selling you an investment loan and tax accountants get rich selling you some hair-brained, tax-based ostrich schemes.

On the other hand, if you avoid all the experts and simply pay off the mortgage first, nobody gets rich except you!

41 Don't bank on your superannuation fund to pay off the mortgage

When you apply for a loan you fill out an assets and liabilities form so the lender can see what you own and what you owe. When I started out as a lender in the early 1980s, lenders didn't consider superannuation as an asset for the purposes of lending applications because it was really just there to provide an income in old age. It was not an asset that lenders counted on to repay loans. The rule was that the loan must be repaid by the borrower from their working income by the time they retired.

Somehow things changed dramatically in the latest lending boom. Now lenders not only count superannuation as an asset, but they also encourage borrowers to borrow more now and use their superannuation payout to pay off the mortgage when they retire. The more the lender can lend you now, the more interest the lender earns, and the more sales commissions the sales reps and mortgage brokers pocket now. They're not worried about your old age—they will get your superannuation fund to pay out the mortgage when you retire. How you survive in your old age is your problem, not theirs!

Banks lent more money and all this extra money pushed house prices higher. According to recent studies, a large and growing proportion of people are using their superannuation funds to pay off their mortgage, either using their payout at retirement, or breaking into their superannuation before retirement under the early release rules. This is certainly not what the superannuation system was intended for. It has been reported that approvals by APRA for early release of superannuation to pay off mortgages rose more than 400 per cent from 2001 to 2006.

Don't be tempted to take on a bigger mortgage with a view to using your superannuation payout to pay it off when you retire. You'll need your superannuation to live off in retirement. You'll probably live 10 or more years longer than your parents did and you'll probably be retrenched or 'downsized' several years younger than they were. This means you will probably need to fund at least 30 years of retirement somehow. You're going to need every cent of your superannuation fund to generate money for living and medical expenses in your retirement.

If you're currently in a mortgage that is due to run until after you estimate you'll retire, you need to make a plan to pay off the mortgage sooner.

42 Let grown-up kids pay part of your mortgage

If you have grown-up kids still living at home, get them to pay rent or board directly into your mortgage. This is much more effective than getting it paid into your bank account because it can't disappear in day-to-day living expenses.

Set up a direct debit out of their bank account or a payroll deduction straight from their salary. It is much easier than trying to get cash out of them each week or month — you'll never win that game! It will be good preparation for them to learn how the real world works.

Make up a list of the total costs of the house, including mortgage, council rates, water, electricity, gas, insurance, repairs and maintenance, gardening and cleaning. Divide the total annual cost into monthly and weekly amounts to give them a better idea of how much running a house costs on a regular basis. This may come as a rude shock to you as well as to the kids!

You can make it an age-based system, with the level of board increasing as they get older each birthday. That way your children can see what lies ahead and it's a powerful motivator for them to start to build a life of their own. The aim is not to push the kids away—you may like having them around. The aim is to prepare them for the real world, as well as to have them appreciate that living in your house is not free and that they should contribute towards it.

43 Consider mortgage contributions instead of presents

At your engagement party or your wedding, try this idea. Rather than guests buying presents, ask them to donate a similar amount of cash instead to go towards your mortgage. To protect their privacy regarding how much each donates, get a friend to collect the cash for you, then hand it over on the night. Guests could also bring their contributions in unmarked envelopes when they arrive. Your friends will appreciate that this is a particularly important goal to you and this will motivate many to make an extra effort to help you out.

An alternative plan might be to ask them to buy you a combined present with part of the cash pool, with the rest to go off the mortgage. This way you get something personal and meaningful plus a nice dent in the mortgage, which will save you many times that amount over the life of the loan.

Every dollar your friends contribute saves about $4.50 in interest on a typical mortgage. If you have 50 people who would normally spend, say, $50 on a present, that's a total of $2500. If you have a 25-year mortgage for $300 000 at 7 per cent, that $2500 in cash paid off the principal balance can save you more than $11 500 in interest and get the mortgage paid off six months sooner. Not bad—a six hour party can knock six months off the mortgage!

44 Downsize—smaller house, smaller mortgage

Over the past century in Australia the number of people per household has been declining steadily, but the average house has been getting bigger, with more and more rooms. Your grandparents probably had four or more children, but the family all lived happily in a tiny three-bedroom cottage with one bathroom and a single living/dining room. These days most families have one or two kids living in a four-bedroom house with two or three bathrooms, a study, family room, rumpus room, media room and so on. But few of us actually have any spare rooms—they're all full of stuff. We don't notice all the stuff as it builds up slowly over time, but it all adds up. That's where all the money goes and that's what gets people into debt. It's no wonder most people feel stressed these days.

People tend to expand to the capacity that they are given. If our houses have six rooms, then we fill up all six rooms. If we have 20 rooms, we fill up all 20. On top of all this stuff, tens of thousands of people rent storage sheds for the things that can't fit in their houses!

If you were showing a Martian around your house, trying to explain what all the rooms were for and what all the stuff was for, you may find yourself making up explanations that not even you believe. We hang onto furniture that has been upgraded years ago, clothes that no longer fit, toys the kids have long grown out of, appliances that no longer work, or are still in their unopened boxes, games that have been played maybe once many years ago, computers that have crashed, exercise equipment that has been rarely used, bikes that are rusted, tools we still haven't used for that project we'll never get around to doing, and so on.

A few houses ago my wife and I sold a large 650 square metre house that we had lived in. We moved into a small, 120 square metre house we owned while our next house was being renovated. We had three shipping containers of contents from the large house put into storage for the year and just lived on what we could fit into one small moving van, which was less than 10 per cent of our total pile of stuff.

We thought it would be a real challenge living on just 10 per cent of our stuff for a year. But after a couple of months we got used to it and we missed hardly anything that was in storage. It was a big eye-opener for us.

If you have a big house and a big mortgage to match, you may find that you can downsize to a smaller, less expensive house with a smaller mortgage and you'll probably feel like a huge weight has been lifted from your shoulders. You'll have less debt, less stuff, a smaller house to keep clean and less stress.

With a smaller house your adult kids will be encouraged to move out, so you can really accelerate your mortgage payments and put the excess into building wealth for your retirement.

45 Trade up houses, but trade down debt

The pattern for many homeowners is to start out with a modest house and a modest mortgage. Then, as their careers or businesses grow, their living expenses also rise and they take on bigger and bigger mortgages to buy bigger and more expensive houses. I often meet people in their forties and fifties with massive mortgages that they have no concrete plan to reduce or pay off. Their only real option is to use their superannuation balance to pay out the mortgage, then try to survive on the government pension and government health system for 30 or 40 years of retirement. They can't downsize to a smaller house to free up cash because the kids are still at home and probably will be for the next 10 or 15 years.

Here's a way of getting out of debt, building wealth and having fun all at the same time. My wife and I have been doing this for more than 20 years and it has contributed to about half our total wealth. Thousands of others have done it successfully as well.

Instead of taking on bigger mortgages for each house, the trick is add real value to the houses so you can sell them, then buy the next house with less debt, not more. With each house you can free up cash, so you can reduce your mortgage size each time and pay off the mortgage completely after a few houses. Here's how to do it.

$ Research your chosen market so you know it inside out. Study the properties and the prices paid. In a few seconds on the internet you can download the address and sale price of every house sold over the past 10 years for just about any suburb across Australia. Walk (don't drive) around the suburb with the list of past prices and get an understanding of all the various pockets or submarkets in your target area. For example, the pockets might be near the railway, around the school, facing the park, along the main roads and so on. Different pockets might also have different land sizes, different sized houses or different style houses built in different eras. Understand what prices the properties go for and why. Go to hundreds of house inspections and dozens of auctions.

$ Research also includes understanding the current and potential buyers and sellers in your chosen market. What sort of people are buying? Why? What features are they looking for? Do the same for sellers. Get to know what is driving property values. Study the factors driving demand for properties in the area, such as employment, transport links, shops, restaurants, schools, hospitals, entertainment, sporting and leisure. Also study the factors driving supply, such as planned developments, zoning and likely future planning trends. You can never do too much research.

$ Specialise, don't diversify. Only by specialising can you build in-depth knowledge so you understand values, know when you are buying for less than the true value and know what types of improvement your target buyers will pay a premium for.

$ Aim for properties where most of the value is in the land and not in the buildings. Focus on rundown houses in great locations. Never forget that well-located land appreciates (if the demand and supply factors are strong), but buildings and improvements always depreciate quickly.

$ Buy for a low price. Work out what the true value is, based on your research, then discount it by at least 20 per cent as your target price. Never get emotional during the buying process. Never compete—if you compete with another bidder you will never get a bargain. If the price gets above target price, simply walk away and look for the next target. 'Once in a lifetime' deals come along every month!

$ Be very selective about what renovations you undertake. Only add things that your target buyers are willing to pay a premium for. In most cases you never get your money back, let alone make a profit. Never pay full retail prices for renovations, fittings and appliances. For example, never buy kitchens or bathrooms via kitchen and bathroom renovation firms. Instead, go straight to the cabinet manufacturers, buy fittings at wholesale auctions and develop a team of reliable tradespeople.

$ Sell when the renovations are still as-new. Renovations, fittings and appliances lose value quickly once you start using them. They also go out of fashion quickly and buyers will not pay a premium for them. Once your renovations are more than a couple of years old, potential buyers will walk in and say, 'What were they thinking? We'll have to renovate!'

$ Finally, it is critical to understand the overall economic cycle and adjust your plans accordingly. The market never booms forever. It always collapses and people with too much debt get burned each time. You will know when a boom has taken prices well above their true value. While everybody else is paying crazy prices, you will be priced out of the market, but that's fine—just wait for the market to fall back (it always does) and buy when all the highly geared people are desperately selling.

46 Try the payout two-step

Here is a trick I have used a number of times over the years with different lenders and it saves several thousand dollars every time.

Most mortgage lenders have early payout penalties when you pay out the loan with a lump sum. It is usually calculated as a number of months interest on the balance at the time of the payout. Lenders don't want you to pay out loans—they want to keep you in debt for as long as possible so they can extract the most money out of you. Find out how the penalties on your loans work by checking the fine print on your loan agreement. If you haven't kept a copy, ask the bank for it.

If you have a 25-year, $300 000 mortgage at 7 per cent, the monthly repayments would be $2120.34. After five years the balance would be $273 486. Let's say that after five years you wanted to pay off the mortgage with money from the sale of a business, sale of a property, or an inheritance. If the payout penalty is three months interest on the balance, you would pay a penalty of $4786 (calculated as $273 486 balance × 7% ÷ 12 × 3 months = $4786), which is nasty. Even a one-month penalty is $1595, which is still too much.

Here's where the payout 'two-step' comes in. Instead of paying out the loan with a single lump sum of the full balance, you make a principal reduction of say $270 000 off the loan, leaving a balance of just $3486. A month later, ring up the lender's call centre and get a payout figure. The penalty will now be calculated on the new tiny balance instead of the previous high balance, so the total three month penalty will be only $61. Even if you are charged a fee of, say, $100 for making the principal reduction (as you do in some loans), you'll still save $4625 in payout penalties.

On some mortgages, the early payout penalty is calculated as a number of months *repayments* (not interest), which is even nastier, but you can still use a version of the 'two-step' here too. Using your cash lump sum, pay off, say, $223 486 of the mortgage, leaving a $50 000 balance and put the other $50 000 into a cash account or into an offset account. Then renegotiate the remaining balance into a 20-year, $50 000 loan at the same interest rate (7 per cent here) so the new repayments are $387.65 per month. (Lenders usually have a minimum loan size of $50 000 for mortgages.) Shortly after, pay out the $50 000 loan with the rest of your cash. The penalty will be based on three of the new much lower repayments ($387.65), instead of the original repayments ($2120.34) on the full $300 000 loan. Even if you pay a renegotiation fee of, say, $500, you will still save nearly $4700 in payout penalties.

You can do this trick only when you are paying out the mortgage with money other than from the sale of the property securing the loan, because there you would have to pay out the whole loan in one hit. But if you are using cash from some other source you can use this method to beat the banks at their own game!

47 Avoid complex mortgage-reduction schemes

Don't be tempted to get involved in complex mortgage-reduction schemes promoted by some mortgage brokers and financial planners. These schemes generally involve shifting money between a combination of different accounts such as lines of credit, credit cards, redraw accounts, offset accounts and often all sorts of other things as well. I have sat through many presentations by planners and mortgage brokers, and most of them are very complex and confusing. Some of the diagrams they use to explain the schemes are so complex they look like they could be plans for a nuclear submarine!

These schemes are often riddled with hidden fees, all paid out of your pocket. Some of them might actually work in theory (if there were no fees), but they generally require extreme discipline on the part of the borrower to stick to the plan. I have seen many cases where the borrowers end up in a worse situation than when they started, as well as paying heavy fees and charges.

It's usually better to stick to a simple plan and put whatever spare cash you do have towards permanent reductions in principal, then don't redraw it or move it around. The more different accounts the money goes through during the process, the more chance you have to accidentally spend it. Probably the most complex plan most people should have is to get their salary paid into an offset account to use spare cash to reduce the interest on the mortgage, then transfer the surplus money each pay cycle to reducing the mortgage principal. This is a good example of where the simplest plan is usually the best.

48 If you have to sell, stay in control

If you're having trouble making your mortgage payments and you have fallen into arrears, the lender will start charging you penalty interest and fees on top of your repayments. If you have exhausted all avenues of negotiation with your lender and still can't make any headway against the mounting debt, there is usually only one way out—sell the house and clear the debt. With the money left over after the sale you can trade down to something less expensive with a much lower mortgage, or you may need to rent for a while.

Hanging on and getting further and further in debt while the penalty interest and fees mount up, and having the lender repossess the house and sell it to clear the debt will usually result in a worse result for both you and the lender. Having a repossession against your name damages your credit rating so it's harder (and more expensive) to get another mortgage for another house. The last thing a lender wants is to have to repossess the house. It means extra legal costs, holding costs and selling costs for them. Mortgagee sales are usually done at the worst possible time in the market. Inevitably, by the time your house gets to the mortgagee auction it will be an empty, deserted, rundown wreck, often damaged by vandals and sometimes with appliances and fittings stripped out by thieves, without you there to look after it and keep your home well presented.

The lender is not interested in maximising the price so you are left with equity after the debt (and penalty interest and fees) is cleared. They will not haggle and negotiate and try to get the price up. The lender will dump the property quickly for the best decent offer they can get on the day. In theory there are laws providing that lenders must maximise their price for your benefit, but this is rarely what happens in the real world, and the borrower is usually in no position to take them to court.

If you are left with no option other than sell the house to clear the debt, it is better to take control of the situation and sell your house yourself before the bank takes possession. If you tell the bank you plan to do this they will usually be happy and support you if the plan is reasonable. You can sell in your own time, on your own terms, with your own solicitor and with your own agent. You will still be in possession of the house during the process so you can make sure it is well maintained and presented. In all cases you would be left far better off than if you let the bank sell it from under you.

Part IV

Credit cards

Credit cards are a great idea if used correctly. The problem is that most people don't use them correctly. The only sensible way to use a credit card is to use it as temporary credit and pay the full balance each month.

It's too easy to run up huge debts and it's getting easier every year. Credit cards allow anybody to buy virtually anything from anywhere in the world any time of the day or night, 365 days a year. And we do!

By the end of 2008, Australians had over 14 million credit cards and we owed a total of $45 billion. That's an average credit card debt of $3000 for every person aged between 18 and 80, or $5900 per household across the entire country.

Credit cards are one of the most expensive ways to borrow money. They carry extremely high interest rates—up to 25 per cent or more once fees are included, even though the card company borrows the money at around 5 per cent. The banks and credit card companies make billions of dollars in profits from credit cards and it all comes out of your pockets!

Every time you use a credit card, ask yourself this question: 'Do I want to look rich or be rich?' That's a very serious question. If you keep spending money you don't have, you will never get out of debt and you will never be rich. Period.

Everybody knows how to get rid of credit card debt. It's no secret: just don't use it to buy anything if you can't pay the full balance each month. Everybody knows that, but it's easier said than done. Fortunately there are some steps you can take to help get off the credit card roundabout forever.

49 Find out how much you spend on credit cards

Do this quick test: estimate how much you spend on your credit cards each month. Get a pencil and write down your estimate on this page. Now get your last half-a-dozen statements for all your cards (or download them from your bank or credit card website) and see how much you really spent. Include all purchases and cash advances you made on all cards. The more past months you can get hold of the better.

From your total spending each month on all cards, work out a monthly average spend and write the actual amount next to your estimate. If you are like most people, the actual amount spent will be at least double the amount you thought you spent each month.

Usually the big amounts are no great surprise. You will see the big items that you know should be there, like the car insurance, house insurance, electricity, water bills and so on. Where most people get a big surprise is the dozens of small items that add up to the bulk of the overall total. These are often a string of tiny amounts that you don't notice at the time, but add up to huge amounts over the month.

Complete a table of the main categories of your spending; for example, groceries, lunches, coffees, pub, lotteries/scratchies, public transport fares, fuel, utilities (water, gas and electricity) and phone. Usually there's a large category of 'other' at the bottom of your list. You need to find out where all this 'other' money goes because this is what will keep you in debt for decades.

50 Choose the right card for your needs

There are many types of credit cards on the market these days, with hundreds of different combinations of features such as interest rates, interest-free periods, fees and loyalty programs.

If you are using a credit card wisely, you will have opted for a long interest-free period and no annual fee. These types of cards usually have high interest rates but that doesn't matter because you will by paying the full balance off each month, so you will carry no core debt that incurs interest.

While you are still trying to get your credit card debt under control, it might pay to transfer to a lower interest rate card to minimise the interest cost over the period while you pay it off completely. If you are doing this you would opt for a nil annual fee, but these usually come with a short interest-free period. This is also fine, because you won't be making any more purchases on the card while you are working on a plan to get rid of the core debt.

Many people fall into the trap of continually switching cards to chase the latest low-interest introductory period offers in the market. It is usually much better to put your energy into paying off the balance, then you won't need to worry about interest rates, special offers and introductory periods because you will never pay any interest ever again.

51 Avoid credit card surfing

Credit card surfing is using one credit card to pay off another card. It is a sure road to financial ruin. I have known people who have explained to me in intricate detail how they shuffle money between cards each month to stay ahead of the game. They have a combination of cards with different interest rates, different interest-free periods, different special offers and different reward schemes—and the money just seems to go around in circles.

I never understand it, but they have convinced themselves that they are saving money somehow. Inevitably when I run into them years later they are either still on the treadmill running frantically to keep ahead of the debt collectors, or they have been declared bankrupt.

If you have to use a credit card cash advance to repay another card or to make a repayment on another debt, this should be a clear message that things are out of control and that something needs to change—*now*. If you have no other options at all, then you can do it once as an absolute last resort. But that should set off alarm bells in your head that are telling you that you need to change the way you handle your money from now on. Unfortunately, for many people, 'just this once' soon turns into a regular habit and it's a very hard habit to break.

52 Never use cash advances

The problem with cash advances on credit cards is that you don't get the normal interest-free period that you get when making purchases on the card. That means that you are paying exorbitant interest rates from the day you take the cash advance. On many cards the interest rate charged on cash advances is even higher than the interest rate on other purchases. Cash advances generally don't count towards rewards points schemes. On top of all this, most card companies charge additional fees for each cash advance. If you add up all the extra interest, fees and charges, cash advances can easily end up costing you an effective annual rate of more than 100 per cent. But millions of people do it without knowing or caring!

Everybody needs cash in their pockets to pay for the dozens of day-to-day expenses that always pop up. Get your petty cash float from the ATM or EFTPOS terminal whenever you need to, but make sure you are withdrawing from your own money sitting in your cash account or transaction account. If there is no cash there, then you need to change your spending habits so you spend only money that you have.

Perhaps the only valid use for cash advances is as a last resort to cover essential expenses for a few days until your next payday. If you ever need to do this, it should be the wakeup call that something is seriously wrong and that you need to urgently change your spending habits. Never get into the habit of using cash advances and never use a cash advance to pay another card or another loan repayment.

53 Cut up your store cards

Store cards are credit cards promoted by major department stores and branded with their store name. They are generally operated by credit card companies, not the store itself. The interest rates on store cards are often higher than on other credit cards because the store believes that somehow your loyalty to its brand will induce you to use its card instead of using other cards when buying items in its store. The store usually gets a cut of the extra interest rates you pay, so it's just another way of getting money out of your pocket and into theirs.

The store is hoping that the fact that you have one of its cards in your purse or wallet will somehow induce you to buy at its store. In reality all it does is put more credit cards within your purse or wallet.

Another motivation for the stores is that it gives them your personal details so they can send you junk mail about supposed sales and even invite you to 'special' shopping sessions. That's the last thing you need—more opportunities to impulse purchase more stuff you didn't need in the first place!

Store cards usually offer interest-free loans to buy things at a particular store. Never use these. When the initial so-called interest-free period is over, the interest rates cut in and they are usually extremely high—often up to 30 per cent per year. And, of course, the store gets a cut of this interest revenue as well. The result is that an item you thought you bought for $1000 supposedly interest-free can end up costing many thousands of dollars. Never let yourself be tricked into one of these.

If you have a store card, cut it up *now*. If you have money owing on it, pay it off as quickly as possible, then cut up the card immediately.

54 Never pay just the minimum amount

If you make just the minimum payment on most credit cards in Australia you will be in debt for the rest of your life—literally!

Credit card companies require a minimum payment that is a percentage of the outstanding balance each month. They want you to stay in debt for as long as possible so they can get fat at your expense. The minimum payment on most cards is just 2 per cent of the balance or $10, whichever is higher, but this is just insane. If you follow this plan it will keep you in debt for the rest of your life—and maybe your children's lives as well!

Here's how. Let's say you have $5000 owing on a credit card with an interest rate of 20 per cent and you make no more purchases or cash advances on the card ever again. If you make just the minimum payment of 2 per cent of the balance or $10 (whichever is higher) each month, it will take you an incredible 798 months or 66.5 years to pay it off in full! It will take 40 years to get the balance down to $1000 and another 25 years to get it down to $100, and you will end up paying a massive $21 627 in interest! As I said — it's insane. If you put your 'vegies on Visa', as the TV ad says, and pay just the minimum balance, you will be paying for today's vegies for the rest of your life!

Twenty years ago the minimum on most cards was 5 per cent of the balance, but now it's just 2 per cent. That's 'innovation' for you — it's sheer madness. This is why credit card debts are so high, and that's what is keeping interest rate margins on credit cards at record levels.

The above numbers are based on a 20 per cent interest rate, but even with a 15 per cent interest rate it will still take 32 years to pay off in full if you pay just 2 per cent or $10 of the balance each month. Don't forget that these numbers assume that you never use the card again. If you use the card to buy anything more and don't pay the full amount each month, it will blow out for even longer.

The easiest way to pay off the credit card debt sooner is to pay off more each month. Instead of paying just 2 per cent of the balance each month, if you can manage to pay off 5 per cent of the balance each month, this will save you a whopping $19 183 in interest and you will get out of debt much sooner. It will still take you 10 years to pay it off fully, but you will get the debt down to $1000 in a little under four years. Figure 4.1 shows the difference between paying 5 per cent of the balance per month compared with paying the minimum 2 per cent per month.

Figure 4.1: paying off the credit card — 5 per cent versus 2 per cent of the balance each month

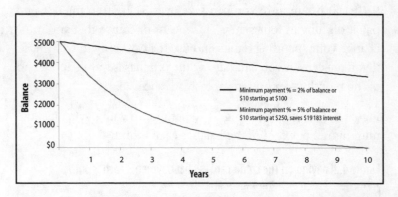

In order to use this plan you can still use the card but you must pay for purchases in full each month and never take cash advances, because they add to the interest bill.

55 Keep payments flat

To use the above plan, you need to increase your payments from the minimum 2 per cent of the balance each month to, say, 5 per cent and you need to find this extra cash from somewhere quickly. For a $5000 credit card debt, this means increasing your monthly repayment from $100 to $250, which may not be possible for many people.

An easier way is to start with the current payment of 2 per cent (which is $100 in the first month) but, instead of reducing the monthly repayments as the balance reduces over time, keep paying off a flat $100 each month. If the interest rate is 20 per cent, this saves you more than $15000 in interest and the balance reduces to $1000 in eight years.

Eight years is still a long time, so if you can find an extra $50 per month (or just $1.64 extra per day) and make the repayments a flat $150 per month, you can save over $19 000 in interest and pay it off fully in four years. This means of course that you must change your spending habits and use the card only to buy things if you are certain you can pay for the purchases in full at the end of the month — and no more cash advances!

Figure 4.2 compares paying $150 per month with paying just the minimum 2 per cent of the balance each month.

Figure 4.2: paying off the credit card — flat payments each month

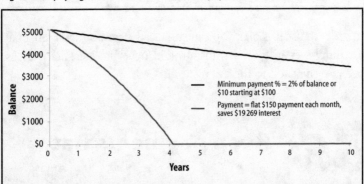

56 *Use direct debits*

Undoubtedly the best way to use a credit card is to have a direct debit set up so the full balance automatically comes out of your bank account when payment is due each month. That way you get the full benefit of the interest-free period each month, and you pay no interest at all, so you're getting an interest-free short-term loan each time you buy something on the card.

However, if you have a core debt on the card of, say, $5000, which you are now trying to pay off, setting up a direct debit from your bank account now will not work because the one-off hit for the full amount of the debt will be too big for the bank account to take. Instead, set up a direct debit of, say, $500 per month from your bank account to the card. You can do this at home via most online banking services and it will pay down the debt much more quickly. Of course, you must now focus every effort on making sure there is at least $500 in the bank account on the day the card payment hits.

Another even more effective direct debt method is to set up the payments to go straight from your pay into the card account. Most payroll systems allow salaries to be split into a number of different accounts and payroll departments are generally happy to help people out.

If the money goes straight from your pay to the card account, it won't go into your bank account first and you won't have a chance to spend it. This is an easy and painless way to pay off the card. Start with a small direct payment amount first and see how easy it is. Then you can increase the payment as you adjust your spending habits.

57 Check every item on statements

It always pays to check every item on your statements. If your credit card company doesn't charge a fee for monthly paper statements then it is usually better to get the paper statements rather than get them emailed online each month. The reason is that with a paper statement you can tick off each item as you check it and you can scribble notes for items for which you need to do more research.

You can always print off emailed statements, but it is just too tempting to quickly 'eyeball' the online statement, say 'it looks okay to me' and delete it. If you receive emailed online statements, print them out and manually check off each item one by one. You may be surprised by what you find.

Often there are items that are incorrect, including:

$ items booked to your card because of mistaken identity

$ items booked by fraudulent operators (often casual cafe and bar staff, or ATM identity fraud)

$ genuine errors where the merchant enters the wrong amount (the 'errors' are usually higher than they should be, rarely lower!).

If you find any problems, ring the card company and they will investigate. The card company is generally liable for fraudulent transactions, so they are usually keen to get to the bottom of any problems.

58 Once you've paid it off, cut it up

Once you've achieved the goal of finally paying off the last of the credit card debt, make sure you don't have to do it again! Don't fall into the trap of getting back into debt straightaway.

This is the financial equivalent of the yo-yo diet. We all have friends or family members who diet and lose weight, then put it straight back on again soon after. We've all heard people say things like, 'I've lost 50 kilos, but it's the same five kilos 10 times!'

I have seen this happen many times with credit card debts. People go to great lengths to change their spending habits and reorganise their affairs to eliminate their high interest rate debts, but if they leave the old credit limit still in place, all too often they drift back into bad habits.

One problem many people have is that, because they have managed to pay off the card once, they let themselves get into debt again because they think that they can pay it off again if they need to. This is the financial equivalent of saying, 'I can give up smoking any time'. They probably can, but inevitably they don't. I run into these people years later and they are still stuck with core credit card debt.

This is especially high risk when refinancing a credit card debt by adding it to a personal loan or a mortgage. After the debt restructure these people still have their credit cards and lines of credit sitting there with nil balances, but they haven't actually changed their habits, they've just shifted the problem to the mortgage. Bad spending habits plus credit cards with credit limits unused equals disaster. For some people it is just too tempting!

It is much better to actually pay off the debt rather than simply hiding it by shifting it to your mortgage. Pay it off, then cut up the card.

59 Consider changing to charge cards

Charge cards are like credit cards, except they need to be repaid in full each month. The most popular charge cards that work around the world are American Express and Diners Club.

When you set up the charge card, you have the option of paying the balance manually or having it automatically debited from another account such as your main transaction account. It is generally best if you set up the automatic payment option. You don't have to remember to pay it off, but you need to ensure there is money in the other account when the payment hits.

Once you realise that you can't carry core debt and the balance must be paid off each month, you soon unconsciously adjust your spending habits so that you use the card only when you know there will be money in your transaction account when the next card bill hits the account. This, of course, is how you should use credit cards as well. Never carry a balance over into the next month.

With charge cards, you still get the benefit of carrying less cash around in your pocket and you get an interest-free period. Another side benefit of charge cards is that they generally have better loyalty reward points schemes than credit cards.

The main disadvantage of charge chards is that some retailers now charge an extra 1 per cent or so on top of the purchase price of the item you are buying, because the merchant fees they pay to the charge card companies are higher than for credit cards. That is no great disadvantage because it is always better to pay cash anyway. With cash you can often negotiate a lower price—cash is king!

60 If you have a charge card, don't take up the credit option

The first card I obtained when I started working was an American Express card and I set up an automatic direct debit from my bank account to pay the full balance each month (my wife started with a Diners card). Back in those days there was no option to carry a balance over to the next month or use a line of credit to pay it off. It was easy back then—you paid off the debt at the end of the month or they took the card off you.

This setup was great training because I learned never to use the card unless I was absolutely certain that the cash would be in the bank account when the card bill hit the account at the end of the month. Over the years I have had credit cards, but I have never ever carried a balance over into the next month, thanks to the training on the charge card.

In the early days of charge cards in Australia the charge card companies had only one card. Now they have dozens of different types of cards. Most of them are credit cards, not charge cards, because they are designed to encourage you to carry a balance from month to month. That way the card company generates interest income from you. Even the charge cards come with options to take up an attached line of credit. It is all very confusing now. For example, American Express has hundreds of little stalls set up in shopping centres and airports with staff selling at least 20 different combinations of Amex cards. If you are going to take the charge card route, stick to a basic card with no credit line attached and where you need to pay the full balance each month.

61 Reduce your credit limits

One of the big problems these days is that technology now allows us to spend money we don't have, 24 hours a day, seven days a week, without even leaving the house. Why not use this same technology to help in your fight against debt?

Once you have been able to reduce your core credit card debt by, say, $1000, ring the card company's call centre and ask them to reduce the credit limit on the card so you don't get back up to the old limit again.

You can also reduce your daily limit on 'pay anyone' and BPAY transactions made from your online banking service ('pay anyone' allows you to make payments direct to any valid account at any bank). You can generally change your daily limits yourself at your computer, without waiting for the bank to do anything.

While you are at it, put a daily limit or overall spending limit on your PayPal account, if you have one. PayPal is used to pay for purchases from online sites such as eBay, and accounts are commonly set up to take the payment from a credit card. It is very easy to get caught up in the online auction process and end up paying more than you initially intended for an item. Reducing the limit is not only a useful safety feature to minimise fraud, but it also helps prevent impulse online purchases.

If you are worried that by reducing your limits you might miss out on that once-in-a-lifetime opportunity, remember an old saying I have been using for years: 'Once-in-a-lifetime deals usually come along every month!' If you come across something that looks like the best thing since sliced bread, don't immediately panic and buy it. Take your time, do your research and you will find a better deal soon pops up.

62 Do leave home without it!

Remember the American Express ads in which Karl Malden says, 'Don't leave home without it'? Well, you should do the opposite with your credit cards. If you are carrying debt on your credit card and not paying off the full balance each month, take the card out of your wallet or purse and leave it at home. Only carry credit cards when you are travelling. By not carrying credit cards with you all the time you eliminate the temptation to buy things when you don't have cash in your bank account.

If you see something you really need you can always use a debit card, where you need to have the cash in the bank account, or go back for it the next day with a credit card. This delay gives you time to shop around for a better deal, as well as time to think about whether or not you really need the item. You can carry debit cards with you at all times because you know that you can use this card only if you actually have the cash in your bank account.

Many people look in their purse or wallet and say 'I can buy this because I have credit cards'. They get themselves into trouble because they should be asking themselves, 'Do I have cash in my bank account to pay for this?' Credit cards are not cash.

Part V

Car loans, personal loans, boat loans and store loans

Car, personal, boat and store loans generally have a similar structure—high interest rates, a fixed loan term, fixed rates for the term of the loan, a principal-and-interest structure, and penalties for paying out the loan early. The lender often takes security over the car, boat, furniture or appliance purchased with the loan, which means if you fall into arrears with your payments, the lender can repossess the items.

The interest rate on these loans depends on the type of security, how much cash deposit you paid, and how the lender views you as a credit risk. Loans from banks secured by new cars are at the lowest rates, sometimes lower than 10 per cent. Loans for used cars attract higher rates because the security is of poorer quality. At the most expensive end of the scale are loans for furniture and appliances, and unsecured personal loans from finance companies. Interest rates for these are often near 30 per cent per year or higher once fees and charges are taken into account.

The golden rule is to never borrow to buy depreciating items, such as cars, furniture, boats and sporting equipment, for personal (non-business) use. Never borrow to pay for living expenses. Always pay cash instead. This is one of the oldest and most basic principles of building wealth. Borrowing to purchase depreciable items used for generating income in a business is another matter (we deal with this in part VII).

Always ask yourself, 'Do I want to look rich or be rich?' If you borrow to buy depreciating non-business assets you'll never be rich—simple as that. The sooner you get rid of these types of debts, the sooner you can get on the path to wealth.

63 Renegotiate, don't refinance

Car, boat, furniture and personal loans are probably the highest interest rate debts you can have besides credit cards. With credit cards, you can pay out the full balance or make any lump sum repayment you like at any time—as long as you have the cash, of course. But car, boat, furniture and personal loans are not like this. They are usually fixed loans over a fixed term, with a fixed interest rate and fixed repayments.

The same principles apply as with principal-and-interest mortgages: the more you can pay off, the less interest you will pay and the sooner you can get out of debt. But with fixed loans it is not as easy to pay off the balance, make lump sum principal reductions or even make extra repayments.

The first thing to do is ring the lender, give your loan account number and ask for the current balance and a payout figure. In most cases you won't have the cash to pay it off in full so you need to know exactly how your loan works on the lender's system. Ask what would happen to your account if your next payment is, say, $50 more than the scheduled repayment, or if you make the next two payments at once. In some loans the extra money will come off the principal balance; in others the loan will go into 'advance' and the excess will not be credited to your account until it is due; and in others the system may reject the payment altogether because it doesn't match the payment due. In the last case the system may treat your loan as 'in arrears' even though you have made more than the required payment.

Tell the lender you would like to accelerate your repayments to pay off the loan more quickly. If you are lucky, the loan system will be able to handle this and you are on your way. Just increase the direct debits each month by whatever you can afford. Even a small increase in your repayments is a good start. Ring up a couple of months later or check the statements to make sure the extra payments are coming off the balance.

If the loan system can't handle larger or extra repayments, or if the loan just goes into advance when extra money is received, then you need to change the loan structure on the lender's system. These types of loans have high interest rates because the lender faces a high risk of loss. The most important thing to the lender is that you keep making repayments regularly, thereby reducing their risk of loss. If you can reduce the balance by even a small lump sum (like $500), or if you can increase your repayments by a modest amount each month (such as $50 more per month) it reduces the risk of loss to the lender and the lender knows it.

Never mention the term 'refinance' in your discussions with the lender. Refinancing a loan means paying out the old loan and setting up a new one. Refinances are generally done at a higher rate than the original loan and you also have to pay the payout penalty on the old loan and maybe a refinance fee on top. But you are not refinancing into a new loan, you are just renegotiating the old loan to pay it off faster. Make sure you keep your existing loan account number so technically it remains the same loan. Also, make sure any lump sum you make comes off the balance and that the lender changes the repayment schedule to accept your new higher repayments.

64 Always pay a cash deposit

The only possible exception to the rule that you should never borrow to buy depreciable non-business assets is your first car. A car is often needed to get to work so it can be essential to earning income. A car used in your own business can be tax deductible; however, for the purposes of this discussion, we are refering to a car for personal use. Your car may still be necessary to get you to work each day, but the cost is not tax deductible because you work for somebody else, not in your own business.

Although you should usually only buy a car using cash, there are some valid reasons for not being able to save up for it; for example, if you are recently divorced, a new immigrant, or have recently suffered an unforeseen financial setback out of your control.

If you have no real option but to borrow to buy a car, minimise the debt by getting the best possible deal on the purchase price and put down as large a deposit as you can. If you have to borrow, buy the cheapest, most efficient car that will do the job reliably. (Remember: do you want to look rich or be rich?)

The problem with borrowing to pay for depreciating items is that the items drop in value much faster than the loan balance does, so you have negative equity for several years. Negative equity means that you owe more than the car is worth. If you had to sell the item because of a financial emergency and pay out the debt, or if you fall behind in payments and the car is repossessed and sold by the lender, you are left with a shortfall you need to pay off somehow.

For example, let's say you bought a new car for $30 000 and took out a $30 000 car loan, which is to be paid off over five years at 15 per cent. Assume the car value depreciates by a typical rate of 25 per cent per year on a diminishing value basis, including 5 per cent depreciation immediately, which is typical for many cars. Figure 5.1 (overleaf) shows the loan balance compared with the car value over the period.

Figure 5.1: car loan balance versus car value

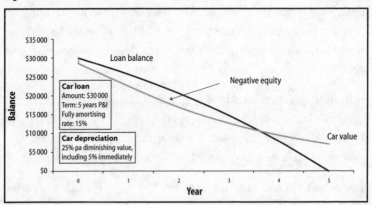

If you had trouble making the repayments and you needed to sell the car any time in the first 3.5 years, the money you'd get by selling the car wouldn't even cover the loan. For example, after two years, you would need to find an extra $3700 plus loan payout penalties (over and above the cash you got for the car) just to pay out the loan. This is a serious problem and leaves you very vulnerable to ending up in even more debt with no way of paying it off and no car to get to work.

In order to avoid the risk of having negative equity any time during the loan term you need to contribute a 20 per cent (in our example that's $6000) cash deposit initially and borrow only $24 000. If you can't afford to do this, you should not be buying the car in the first place. A much safer plan is to buy a cheaper car so that you can contribute at least a 20 per cent cash deposit and borrow less.

65   Never buy new

One simple way to pay less and borrow less for a car is never to buy new. Whether it is your first car or your tenth, whether you're buying a Fiat or a Ferrari, there is rarely a good reason to buy new, especially if you have to borrow. The main buyers of new cars are corporate and government fleets. They buy new because it's not their money, it's shareholders' and taxpayers' money. In the case of your personal car it's your money, so don't throw it away. If you're borrowing, it's not even your money you're throwing away. It's the lender's money and the lender will hound you until you pay back every cent of it, plus interest!

As with all depreciable items, as soon as you drive a new car out of the showroom it drops in value by at least 5 to 10 per cent. After just one year the values drop at least 20 to 30 per cent. Let's say you plan to keep the car for, say, seven years. If a car is going to last seven years, then it is going to last eight years, so you are going to get the same seven years of use out of a new car as you would out of a car that is one year old when you buy it. A one-year-old car costs 20 to 30 per cent less than the equivalent new car, but when you sell or trade it in seven years later, the trade-in price of a seven-year-old car is virtually the same as an eight-year-old equivalent car. So you can save 20 to 30 per cent upfront and the car will last the same as a new one, and trade or sell for virtually the same value.

Of course, don't use this 20 to 30 per cent saving to buy a more expensive car! Borrow less.

Some people are serial new car purchasers—they 'must' trade up to the latest model every three or four years. Prices of new cars are always rising and, because the trade-in value of the car drops faster than the balance on the loan, their level of debt increases progressively over the years instead of reducing. It's a treadmill that's hard to get off. Thousands of suburban streets all over Australia have someone who has a reputation for always buying the latest Ford or BMW. For a lot of people, their self-esteem and sense of identity is tied up in the new cars they buy. A small proportion may be paying cash each time, but the vast majority are borrowing, and it's a sure road to financial ruin. The sooner you can break this cycle the better.

Don't kid yourself—a car is never an investment!

66 Don't self-insure

If you have no comprehensive car insurance and someone runs into your car or steals it you can be left with no car to drive to work and no insurance payout to buy another one. Lack of insurance can be a major financial setback, so if you can't afford to buy comprehensive insurance for the car, you can't afford the car. Comprehensive insurance enables you to get back on the road quickly without going into debt to buy a replacement car.

The alternative to comprehensive insurance is called self-insurance, which is the term for taking on the insurance risk yourself instead of paying an insurance company to do it. This is fine in theory, but it means you must put away the same amount as the insurance premium each year into a savings account, so that you have the cash ready if something goes wrong.

In practice, it is just too hard. If you don't pay the insurance premium to an insurance company, the money disappears in everyday spending. It is much easier and more effective to pay the insurance premium so you are covered.

Car dealers make only about one-third of their money from selling cars. The other two-thirds of their revenue comes from the sales commissions they make on the finance and insurance they sell on the cars. They know that selling high-rate finance and insurance is easy because the buyers are distracted and focused emotionally on the car. Never buy finance from a car dealer when you buy the car. If you can't pay cash, shop around for finance before you go shopping for a car. Once you've found the car you want, most banks can arrange payment to any dealer within 24 hours.

Also, never buy insurance from a car dealer without shopping around first. Most are from high-rate insurance companies, and the premium is loaded up with massive sales commissions paid to the car dealer. When you buy a car, if it is registered it will already have the compulsory third-party insurance, but shop around later for comprehensive insurance and you can generally save up to half the premium.

67 Don't use store loans

Store loans are those 'pay no interest for x years' loans sold by furniture, appliance and electronics retailers to get people to buy things they can't afford. The retailer is paid upfront when you buy the goods and you end up owing much more to a finance company (most are American). These deals sound great, but they can cost you a fortune and keep you in debt for many years. You can end up paying many times the original cost of the item. By the time you finally finish paying off the massive interest, fees and charges, the item you bought will probably be long gone to the rubbish tip.

The fine print differs from loan to loan, but generally it works like this: during the interest-free period you pay no interest, but it is still being calculated, and is being capitalised and added to the loan. The finance company doesn't call it interest, it calls it 'credit charges', but it's the same thing. At the end of the interest-free period you start paying this much bigger amount off at a very high interest rate. If you are just one day late on just one payment, you trigger a clause that says the whole amount of the loan is due immediately and you are liable for an exorbitant interest rate (usually around 30 per cent per year) for the whole term, including the period you thought was supposed to be interest-free, plus a whole load of penalty fees and charges on top.

The finance companies are very quick to offload your debt to private debt collectors and that's when they can really start to make your life hell. Debt collectors often make threatening phone calls to the borrower's home at night, and they often tell the borrower's work colleagues, friends and even the neighbours that they owe money. It can get very ugly very quickly.

If you have avoided these nasty loans so far, congratulations, keep it this way. Remember, if you can't pay cash for something, you can't afford it.

If you have one or more of these loans, be extremely careful. Double-check and triple-check the exact amount of payments and their due dates. Mark these in your diary or calendar, put prominent notices on your fridge, on your bathroom mirror—everywhere. Ring the lender *today* to ask them about how you can pay off the full amount or make extra repayments. These are the most expensive types of loans (apart from credit card cash advances), so make it an urgent priority to clear these debts as soon as possible.

68 If you fall into arrears, tell your lender as soon as possible

If you fall behind in your loan repayments, your lender usually has the right (under the contract you signed) to charge extra penalty interest and fees, and cancel the loan. If you get too far behind, the lender has the right to repossess its security (your house in the case of a mortgage, your car in the case of a car loan, your boat in the case of a boat loan) and sell it from under you. If there is still money left owing after selling the security asset, or if there is no security the lender can sell, the lender can take you to court and get a court judgement against you for the balance (plus even more fees and charges) and then seize your other possessions and sell them, too.

If you have trouble making repayments, it is natural to avoid telling the lender anything. This is war and lenders are the enemy! Borrowing money for non-business purposes is a necessary evil and lenders are cunning, always trying to get you into more debt, and trying to charge extra fees, commissions and higher interest rates whenever they can get away with it. If your income falls or if your financial circumstances worsen, the last thing you would want to do is show the enemy any sign of weakness by telling them about it.

Everyone has the odd bad month when the money is temporarily tight. However, if your situation doesn't improve after a few months and you are really having trouble keeping up, cooperating with the lenders can bring the best outcome for both parties. If you keep falling behind, extra interest and fees continue to build up and it is very hard to get out from under the pile of debt. It is time to recognise that you need to change your tactics and meet with the enemy.

The first step is to call the lender and explain that you want to find a way to make more manageable repayments. This is an important step because it lets the lender know that you are not hostile and that you genuinely want to keep making payments. If you explain what you have done to rectify the problem and tell them that you simply can't make the full repayments, in most cases the lender will be prepared to agree to a revised repayment plan. The key is to make sure you stick to the new repayment plan. It is better to start small and stick to it, than to start big and fall behind again. You need to show the lender that you can stick to an agreed plan.

If you cooperate and approach the lender first, often the lender will agree to waive further penalty interest and fees, or limit them to a certain amount for as long as you stick to the new payment plan. From the point of view of the lender, getting any payments from you is better than getting nothing at all and having to resort to legal measures. Nobody wants to call in the lawyers (not even bankers like lawyers—nobody likes lawyers except other lawyers!)

69 Get the credit bureau to limit more lending

Before approving any loan, lenders obtain a credit report on the applicant from a credit bureau. The credit bureau keeps a file on all borrowers, including how much you applied for, and any arrears (late payments), defaults, or court judgements against you.

One way to virtually guarantee that no lender extends more credit to you is to contact the credit bureau and ask to put a voluntary note on your file not to extend further credit until you withdraw the note from the file.

This is a radical step. It's like stomach stapling for your debt—even if you wanted to borrow more you can't, because lenders would be warned away.

You can always have this voluntary file note removed at a later date when you are comfortable with your ability to handle more debt, although you may find that you never need to remove the note because you have cured your addiction to debt.

The primary consumer credit bureau in Australia and New Zealand is Veda Advantage Ltd. The contact details are:

$ Australia: <www.mycreditfile.com.au>
Phone: 1300 762 207

$ New Zealand: <www.mycreditfile.co.nz>
Phone: 0800 692 733

70 Celebrate each win

Every time you pay off a debt you should reward yourself with a small celebration. It might be a dinner or a night out with family or a few friends. If it's with a group of friends you may find that they are also working to pay off debts of their own and you have your own little support group. This can be a very powerful motivator and a good way to keep each other on track.

Book the restaurant well in advance so you have a specific deadline to work towards. If you are using your debt calendar to prioritise and plan for paying off your debts, pick a date that is a couple of weeks after the target date on your calendar. That way you can handle any last-minute surprises, which always crop up. You also have a couple of extra weeks to save up the cash to pay for the reward.

Of course, you must always pay for the reward with cash—and don't even think about cheating by using a cash advance on your credit card! The last thing you want to do is get back into debt again. You will find there is a real sense of satisfaction in being able to pay cash.

Part VI

Investment loans

This part covers the most common types of investment loans—loans to buy investment properties and shares. The rules that apply to these loans are slightly different from the rules that govern other kinds of debt. This is because the interest on the loans is generally tax deductible if the loan is used to purchase assets that are intended to generate taxable income.

The aim of investment loans is to use debt wisely in order to build net wealth, but the ultimate goal is the same as with personal debts: to get rid of the debt in the most cost-effective and tax-effective way possible.

71 Use principal-and-interest loans for investment properties

A large proportion of property investors in Australia use interest-only loans to buy investment properties, but I have always favoured principal-and-interest (P&I) loans. The reason most investors use interest-only loans is because the repayments are lower, so they can borrow more money for a given level of income. For example, if you are borrowing $300000 at 7 per cent, repayments on a 25-year P&I loan are $2120.34 per month. But repayments on an interest-only loan for $300000 are only $1750 per month, which means you can borrow 20 per cent more.

Many investors make the mistake of assuming that the higher repayments on P&I loans means more tax benefits; however, only the interest portion of each repayment is tax deductible.

If you are using investment properties to build wealth for your retirement, you should aim to get out of debt altogether (or reduce debts substantially) by the time you retire. If you are using interest-only loans on your properties, your overall level of debt doesn't reduce over time, so you generally need to sell a few properties in order to use the cash to retire debt on the properties you retain. This usually means paying capital gains tax on the properties you sell.

On the other hand, if you are using P&I loans, you will be paying off the debt gradually each year, so by the time you retire the overall debt burden will be much more manageable and you can retire without having to sell any properties. Think of the P&I plan as another forced saving mechanism that uses spare cash flow to build more net wealth over the long term.

The interest-only plan enables you to buy more properties now, but you take on more debt and incur more capital gains tax later on. Under the P&I plan, you buy fewer properties, but have lower debt, pay lower or nil capital gains tax and carry less risk during the plan.

72 Avoid fixed-rate loans for rental properties

A large proportion of investment property loans in Australia are fixed rate (a much larger proportion than for owner-occupier loans.) The theory is that rent is a more-or-less fixed constant over time, so it is better to match it with fixed or constant loan payments.

This is an illusion. Rents do not remain constant. They don't even rise smoothly over time by the inflation rate. Rents on most investment properties vary significantly with the ups and downs in the economic cycle, whether they are residential properties (houses and flats), retail (shops), commercial (offices) or industrial (warehouses and factories). In fact, residential rents tend to be the most volatile type of investment property (with the exception of tourist properties), because residential rents are generally set for periods of one year at the most at a time. Most other main types of property tend to have rents fixed for several years at a time, with industrial properties having the longest leases (often 10 years). The longer the lease period, the longer the fixed-rate loan period can be.

For residential properties (which are by far the most popular form of property investment), it generally makes more sense to stick to variable-rate mortgages, because repayments are a better match with the rental revenues. Residential rents tend to rise sharply in economic booms when mortgage interest rates are also rising (assuming you have chosen a good location where demand is strong). In the economic slowdowns and recessions that follow, interest rates fall and rental rates also fall or stay flat at best for several years. Vacancies rise, so net rental revenue falls at the same time as variable interest rates are falling.

Many thousands of people buy investment flats and houses near the top of the housing price cycle when the economy is booming, interest rates are high and everybody else is also buying, and they take out fixed-rate mortgages to protect against further rate rises. Not only is this the worst time to buy investment properties, but it is also the worst time to lock in fixed rates. You will be locked into paying high boom-time fixed rates, so you won't get the benefit of falling interest rates in the slowdown that follows.

Being locked into high fixed rates during a slowdown with falling rental revenues can often put pressure on cash flows at the same time as your other income may be under pressure from your work or business. This can often lead to the forced sale of investment properties at the worst time in the cycle.

73 Avoid lines of credit for investment properties

Investing generally involves buying assets (such as property or shares) for their long-term growth potential. Many investors use a line of credit secured by their house to buy long-term assets, but this is generally not the most effective method of financing.

When investing in long-term assets it is generally better to use a fixed-term loan because the interest rates are usually lower than lines of credit. With a line of credit you are paying extra for the ability to draw down and repay amounts whenever you want. This benefit is usually of little use to long-term property or share investors, because investment properties and shares usually involve borrowing a fixed amount upfront for several years.

Line-of-credit mortgages generally have interest rates of at least 0.5 per cent to 1 per cent above basic no-frills P&I term loans. This doesn't sound much, but it will eat up a significant proportion of your investment yield. For example, if your rental property is yielding, say, 5 per cent gross rent, with 25 per cent of rent going in expenses, your net rental yield before interest is 3.75 per cent. A saving of just 0.5 per cent interest rate on the loan boosts your net rental yield and cash-flow before tax by 13 per cent on the property. Likewise, if you are borrowing 100 per cent to buy shares with a dividend yield of, say, 4 per cent, an interest saving of 0.5 per cent will boost your net yield and cash-flow before tax by 12.5 per cent.

Another reason to avoid lines of credit for long-term investment plans is that they have no built-in mechanism for repaying the debt over time, whereas a P&I loan does.

Lines of credit are best suited to people who need irregular amounts of cash at irregular intervals and are willing to pay the extra interest rate for this flexibility. A line of credit is like a secured overdraft, so it is best used like an overdraft; that is, for occasional irregular, temporary cash flow needs, not core debt. One good use for a line of credit is paying deposits on investment properties, as long as you then finance the settlement of the purchase with a long-term loan at a cheaper rate than the line of credit.

74   *Use your tax refund*

Borrowing to buy shares or property can be an effective way of building long-term wealth; shares have a number of tax advantages. In Australia the relatively high dividend yields, together with dividend franking rules, make borrowing to buy shares or property especially attractive because the cash flow after tax is usually positive even if borrowing up to 100 per cent of the value of the shares you buy. In addition, share buybacks and capital returns can also generate tax benefits.

In the case of property, there are also tax benefits in the form of depreciation allowances and capital works allowances. Investors in property trusts also receive these deductions passed though the trust to them, as well as other tax breaks arising from tax credits.

The operation of tax rules and tax breaks on various kinds of income from shares and property investments mean that most geared-up investors receive tax refunds in most years. In particular, salaried investors who have income tax already deducted from their pay receive a nice bonus in the form of a tax refund from the tax office. Many investors see this as a bonus to be blown on expenses or on luxuries such as a holiday. By all means, reward yourself, but make sure most of your tax refund goes towards building long-term wealth. If you put the tax refund to work by reducing the mortgage, you will be debt-free sooner and be able to leave work to live off your investment earnings sooner.

75 Don't use deposit bonds

The deposit bond was another so-called innovation of the last lending boom. It enabled people to commit themselves to hundreds of thousands of dollars of debt by putting just a couple of hundred dollars on their credit cards, instead of actually saving a deposit. Deposit bonds turned what used to be a serious decision people took years to think about, plan and save up for into an impulse purchase they could put on a credit card in a few minutes. An insurance company does a quick credit check on you and sells you a deposit bond that you can use instead of a cash deposit to buy a property. When settlement is due, the insurance company coughs up the cash deposit to the vendor and collects the money from you or your lender. If you don't have the few hundred dollars it costs for the deposit bond, no worries, they take credit cards. How easy is this!

There are circumstances where using a deposit bond can be a good idea; for example, when your deposit for the property is tied up in a bank term deposit and where the cost of the deposit bond is less than the interest penalty for breaking the term deposit early. But if you don't have the full deposit saved and ready to hand over at settlement, never use a deposit bond.

Too many people fall into the trap of thinking it's an easy way to buy a property. Many times I've heard people say things like 'Let's buy a few flats off the plan and stick it all on the credit card! We'll "flick" (on-sell) them before the settlements are due and make a fortune!' The value of new flats bought off the plan (before they are built) will often rise in the boom even though they aren't even built yet. In the frenzy of the boom it sometimes works a couple of times so it is easy to become greedy and do it again with more flats each time. Then the boom stops and the value of the flats falls. The problem is that you can't sell them before settlement and you are forced to borrow the full amount of the purchase price in order to settle the purchases.

Even if you bought just one flat off the plan with a deposit bond, suddenly you are forced to borrow the full price of, say, $500 000 to buy the flat, which is now worth maybe $450 000 or less on settlement once the boom is over. If you don't have enough equity in your own home, or if you don't have the income to cover both loans, you won't be able to raise the $500 000, so you are sued by the property developer for the full price. Even if you do have equity in your home and sufficient income to support the extra loan, you are stuck with an empty flat nobody wants, in a building full of empty flats nobody wants. Many thousands of people lose not only the flats they 'bought' with the deposit bonds, but their homes as well.

I have seen this same pattern with off-the-plan flats over three different boom-and-bust cycles, and it's never pretty. Deposit bonds have made the problem even worse.

76 Don't borrow for the holiday house

Holiday houses, beach houses and hobby farms should be seen as lifestyle expenses and should not be bought with borrowed money. They shouldn't be seen as investments unless they are rented out for the whole period you are paying interest.

The interest and other operating expenses are tax deductible against your income only for the portion of the year that the house is actually rented out or available for rent at realistic market rates. For example, let's say your interest bill for a holiday house is $15 000 per year and the holding costs (council rates, land tax, utilities and maintenance costs) are another $5000 per year, making total running costs $20 000 per year. If you rent the place out and/or have it listed with agents for a realistic market rent for only 10 weeks of the year, then only 19 per cent (10 ÷ 52) of the interest and expenses are tax deductible for that year.

Many thousands of people assume wrongly that they can claim a tax deduction for the whole of the interest and expenses, even if they use the place themselves. They take on debt to buy the place, wrongly assuming the tax deductions will help pay the interest and running costs. It is a recipe for disaster because it is easy to pay too much by buying at the wrong time.

It is generally a good rule never to buy a holiday house while you are on holidays. If you are planning to buy for cash, it will take you several years to save. This gives you plenty of time to research the market and also minimises the risk of making an impulse purchase. If you have done your research and have carefully selected an area to target, go there during the off-season and you will nearly always be able to buy for a lower price because you aren't competing with other holiday makers.

There are definitely wrong times and right times to buy holiday houses. The wrong time to buy is when the economy is booming, when interest rates are rising, and when all your friends and colleagues are also buying them. This is where many people get caught up in the boom and pay too much, because the prices of holiday houses can rise rapidly in economic booms.

The best time to buy holiday houses is in economic slowdowns that inevitably follow booms. This is when the unemployment rate is rising, interest rates are falling, and your friends and colleagues are selling. In downturns, holiday house prices suffer first and by the greatest amount. This is the time to buy—with cash, and after you have done plenty of research.

77 Borrow in the same currency as your income

Many people buy investment properties overseas. For example, it is popular for Australians to buy properties in New Zealand and for New Zealanders to buy properties in Australia. Further afield, the UK, US, Europe, Hong Kong and Indonesia are also places where many Australians and New Zealanders have bought investment properties. Many people from all over Asia who came to Australia as students and now live and work here have bought properties in their country of origin.

When you buy an investment in another country you are not only taking a risk on the property value in its local currency, but you are also taking a risk that the currency moves against the currency of the country in which you live and work. For example, if you are living and working in Australia and have property in Hong Kong, you are exposed to the risk of changes in the value of Hong Kong properties in Hong Kong dollars, but you are also exposed to the risk of changes in the exchange rate between Hong Kong dollars and Aussie dollars.

One of the golden rules with borrowing is to try to match the interest expense with the revenue from the investment and to match the currency of the loan with the currency of the asset. This means borrowing in the same currency as the investment income. Many investors borrow in the currency with the lowest interest rates to try to save money, but are burned badly when the currency moves against them.

For example, many investors with properties in Indonesia, Thailand and Malaysia who borrowed against their houses in Australia with Australian loans in Australian dollars were burned badly when the Asian currencies collapsed in the late 1990s Asian currency crisis. In Australian dollar terms, the value of the foreign currencies crashed by a half or even three-quarters in some cases and so did the value of their investment properties. The problem was that they still owed the full amount of the loan in Australian dollars to the Australian bank. Had they borrowed in the same currency as the investment, the value of the loan would have fallen with the currency. The property would be worth less, but they would owe less on it, so they would have 'hedged' (or protected) their currency risk.

If buying an overseas investment, you don't have to set up a new relationship with a bank in the foreign country to get a foreign currency loan. Most Australian banks can organise loans in dozens of different currencies these days. You can also borrow in Australian dollars, then hedge the currency, but the bank fees and charges for the hedging service usually make you no better off than when you started. You don't need to pay for additional hedging. You are already hedged because the investment income is in the same currency as the loan.

The same rule works in reverse. It is very tempting for local borrowers to borrow in foreign currencies at lower interest rates, when their assets and incomes are in local dollars. For example, thousands of Australian farmers were induced by banks to borrow to fund their Australian farms using Swiss franc loans at very low interest rates in the 1980s and 1990s. Australian banks were offering Swiss franc loans at interest rates of 3 per cent compared with Australian dollar loans at 15 per cent or more. It was an easy sell for the banks and many farmers jumped at the chance to save money this way.

Their farm assets and farm incomes were in Australian dollars but they paid very low interest rates in Swiss francs. It seemed too good to be true. The problem was that when the Aussie dollar halved in value against the Swiss franc between the early 1980s and late 1990s, the farmers ended up owing double the amount they borrowed. Many hundreds defaulted and ended up owing three or four times the amount they borrowed, once penalty interest and fees were added on top.

If you currently have a loan in a different currency to the asset and income, talk to your bank about trying to better match the currency of the loan and interest expense to the currency of the asset and income. What looks like an interest saving now can quickly turn to disaster as currency markets can move very quickly.

78 Beware the margin on share loans

There are two main ways of borrowing to buy shares: margin loans (where the lender takes security of the shares purchased) and loans secured by other assets, mainly real estate.

Specialist margin lenders are owned by or associated with stockbroking firms. As no extra security is taken by the lender, you don't need to take out a mortgage on your house or other property. Interest rates on margin loans are generally a couple of percentage points above the rates on loans secured by real estate. Margin lending tends to be a rapidly growing sector during stock market booms. In fact all the extra money borrowed to buy shares just pushes the boom higher towards the inevitable collapse that follows every boom.

One potential advantage of margin loans is that each margin lender has restrictions on what stocks it will lend against, the maximum loan-to-value ratio (LVR) it will lend against each stock and the minimum level of diversification. These restrictions are a natural protection for borrowers and the lender. The problem is that in the booms many margin lenders tend to get caught up in the boom mentality by relaxing the rules and encouraging people to borrow very high amounts against virtually any stock. In the crash that inevitably follows, thousands of borrowers, and even margin lenders and stockbroking firms, are sent to the wall.

Aside from the higher interest rate, the other main disadvantage of margin loans is the dreaded margin call. If the value of your shares drops below their pre-set limit, you need to top up your security with cash to make up the shortfall. If you can't find the cash immediately, the lender will sell enough shares to bring the loan down to within its limit. This generally happens at the worst time in the market and can cause further falls in share prices.

The other way of borrowing to buy shares is to borrow using a loan secured by real estate such as your house or an investment property. Many people consider this riskier because you could lose your house if share prices drop too far. In practice it is no riskier than a margin loan. When you sign any loan contract, you become personally liable to the lender. If you don't pay up, the lender will go after any and all of your assets, including the shares and your house, so your house is not safe with a margin loan either.

The higher interest rates on margin loans compared with loans secured by real estate makes a huge difference to your overall investment returns. With a term loan secured by real estate you don't face the risk of margin calls, so you don't have to constantly worry about the values falling below some arbitrary level. Shares are a long-term investment and you can focus on your long-term investment plan without having to keep looking at the share prices every day as you do with a margin loan.

The main disadvantage of borrowing against real estate is that you need to get your mortgage lender involved to approve the additional loan. There may be additional costs of mortgage stamp duty and application fees, but these costs are usually minor compared with the huge savings in interest with the lower interest rate if it's secured by real estate.

The only advantage of margin loans is that you can use them even if you have no equity in your house or other hard assets to borrow against. But this is not an advantage at all. If you have no equity in your house or other hard assets, then you should not be borrowing to buy shares. It is better to start small without borrowing, then gradually build your knowledge and expertise in the market over time. There are no shortcuts to building wealth.

79 Use dividends to pay off the principal on share loans

Borrowing to buy shares can be an effective way to build long-term wealth. In Australia, the relatively high dividend yields, together with dividend franking rules (tax rebates for company income tax already paid by the company) make it especially attractive. The cash flow after tax from borrowing to buy a broad basket of shares is often positive even if you're borrowing up to 100 per cent of the value of the shares you buy.

Even though company share prices fluctuate up and down wildly from day to day, month to month and year to year, the underlying company earnings are generally less volatile, but still fluctuate up and down with the economy. On the other hand, the dividends, which provide you with cash flow to make the loan payments, are far more consistent. There will be the occasional year when dividends fall, but in most years the cash dividends from a diversified share portfolio rise along with overall economic growth and inflation.

As dividends rise in most years, the positive cash flow from the plan also grows over the years. The best way to use this excess cash flow is to start paying off the principal on the share loan, especially if you are still working and don't need the extra cash flow straight away. By using the cash flow to pay off debt and build your equity instead of just spending it, you are setting yourself up for an earlier and more prosperous retirement.

Also, by using part or all of the dividends and tax refunds to pay off the loan balance each year, you avoid having to sell down part of your portfolio (and pay capital gains tax) when you want to stop work and live off the dividends. One way to create your own forced savings plan to progressively pay off the principal is to use a principal-and-interest loan instead of an interest-only loan. This is particularly effective if you are borrowing less than 100 per cent of the cost of the shares, because the plan can often still be cash-flow positive after tax from day one.

Part VII

Small business debts

Running a small business is big business in Australia: according to the Australian Bureau of Statistics, 1.9 million Australians operate a small business, which is one in every six people aged between 20 and 60. Of these, 1.2 million are sole operators, including tradespeople, medical professionals and consultants. Unlike the accumulation of debt in personal finances, debt is not always a bad thing when running a business, because it can be used to finance assets that generate income, and the interest on business debt can be tax deductible.

Although debt can be useful in a business, it needs to be used wisely and managed carefully. The majority of small businesses fail within just a few years, primarily because of poor cash-flow management, which is often caused by poor management of debt. Most small businesses are really one-person shows operated by a tradesperson, professional or service worker, where the business has little or no value to a buyer and can't be sold to pay off debts. In these cases it is critical to have a plan for minimising and paying off debts using business cash flows.

80 Get your personal finances sorted before starting a business

Don't start or buy a business until your personal finances are under control. Many people look to start or buy a small business as a way to solve financial problems, but for most people this is a sure road to more financial problems.

Whether buying a business or starting a new one from scratch, almost every new business owner underestimates the amount of cash needed. Because everybody has limited cash reserves, this usually means that businesses end up taking on more debt or using up credit limits more quickly than they planned, and this can restrict growth.

One of the most important lessons in running a business is that profitability is very different from cash flow. A business may be very profitable in the sense that it receives higher prices for goods or services than they cost to provide, but it can still go broke because of poor management of cash flow. Most small businesses fail in the first year or so because of poor cash flow management, not through lack of profitability.

Running a business requires much more financial discipline and control than running your personal finances, so you are really starting behind the eightball if you are having trouble with finances before you even get into the business.

Use the steps outlined in this book to get out of personal debt before you take the leap into a business. While you are paying off your personal debts, use this time to research your new business idea in detail. The extra time you take on research now will give your business a much greater chance of success when you do take the plunge.

81 Keep business finances separate

Always keep your business finances separate from your personal finances. Business finances include revenues from customers, payments to suppliers, tax payments and refunds, purchases of capital items and borrowings. The business should have its own separate transaction account, cheque book, credit card if you need one, and loan accounts.

Interest on personal debts is not tax deductible, but interest on debts used to generate assessable income in a business generally is. It is critical to keep accounts separate so that the Tax Office can clearly see the business's revenues and costs. If the accounts are mixed, you run the risk of the Tax Office not allowing all or any of your legitimate tax deductions. One mistake many small business owners make is to mix personal expenses with business expenses, then try to claim deductions for the personal expenses. Often this can continue for many years, but when they are finally audited by the Tax Office, the fines and penalties can be very heavy.

Another advantage in keeping finances separate is that it is easier to organise things to ensure that you are using spare cash generated by the business to pay off personal debts first, before paying off business debts.

82 Use your business plan

Most businesses have a business plan. That's the document you put together for the bank to get the loan at the outset, then filed away and forgot about.

Your business plan should be a working document that is kept up-to-date to reflect the current state of the market, the industry, your competitors, your current marketing plan, staffing plan, budget and financial plan.

Use your business plan to regularly check your progress on the financial front, including managing debt and reducing debt over time. Use your business plan to set targets and check your progress on things such as:

$ type of financing—the mix of debt and equity in your business

$ type of debt—are you using the best sources of finance for each financial need?

$ interest rates—are you getting the best rates and terms from your lenders?

I spent many years as a lender at large international banks, lending to all types of business, from small one-person bands to huge multinationals. A business with a well-researched, up-to-date, concise business plan always gets a better reception and better rates and terms from lenders than a business with a vague plan or scribbles on the back of an envelope. If you take your business seriously and treat it like a big business, your lenders will too.

83 Don't make capital purchases using the overdraft

Capital equipment includes any asset used by the business to generate revenue over several years, such as machinery, computers, vehicles, office furniture and shop fitout. Capital equipment is usually expensive so most businesses borrow money to buy it.

The best way to finance a capital asset is to spread the cost of the item over the period it will be used to generate revenue.

For many types of specialised equipment and machinery, the manufacturer or distributor will have a relationship with a finance company that finances businesses purchasing their equipment. Because they specialise in the equipment they usually offer interest rates lower than a general finance or leasing company (and usually much lower than bank overdraft rates). As they specialise in the equipment and understand the secondary market, they often also undertake to buy the equipment back for a set price at the end of the lease.

If you bought existing capital items with your overdraft, you're paying far too much in interest for the items. In many cases the specialist finance companies associated with the original manufacturer or distributor of the equipment are prepared to refinance your secondhand equipment, especially if you bought it from them initially, and the equipment is still used in the business and only part way through its useful life. When refinancing used equipment, the interest rate is higher than for new equipment, but still significantly lower than bank overdraft rates.

By refinancing existing equipment you can free up cash and use it to reduce the high interest rate overdraft.

84 Don't extend your lease term too long

When financing business equipment on lease, make sure the lease term does not exceed the expected life of the asset. The longer the lease term is, the lower the lease payments, so it is tempting to push the lease term out to ease cash flow in the short term. Table 7.1 shows the lease payments for different terms for an asset costing $100000 with a 30 per cent residual and an interest rate of 10 per cent. The residual is the lump sum payment at the end of almost all finance leases. In theory the residual should be the estimated resale value of the item at the end of the lease term, but in practice it can be anywhere between 10 and 60 per cent of the purchase price. Residuals are discussed in more detail in the next section.

Table 7.1: lease terms and monthly lease payments

Lease term	Monthly lease payment
3 years	$2488
4 years	$2009
5 years	$1723
6 years	$1534

If the expected life of an asset is, say, four years, don't be tempted to take a five year lease to make the lease payments lower. The cash flow is slightly better each year over the period, but you're not building up more net equity in the business.

If the equipment lasts as long as expected (four years) you will need to replace the asset before the end of the lease term. The asset will be worth only its salvage value of $30000, but the lease payout figure after four years will be $46917, leaving a substantial cash shortfall you will need to find from somewhere.

Having artificially long leases gives business owners a false sense of profitability. Many get a rude shock at the end of an asset's life when they realise that the business has not been profitable at all, once the full cost of the lease is added in. If you already have leases in this position, talk to your leasing company about refinancing to terms that better match the life of the assets, so that cash flow planning and profitability planning is made easier.

Another advantage of shorter lease terms is the tax benefits. With leases, unlike other principal-and-interest financing methods, the whole of the lease payments are tax deductible (not just the interest portion). Higher tax deductions mean greater tax benefits sooner, which can be reinvested in the business or used to pay down debt.

85 Avoid high lease residuals

Another trap to avoid is setting high residuals on leased equipment. The lease residual is the final lump sum or 'balloon' payment due at the end of the lease. The aim is to set the residual so it more or less matches the salvage (or resale) value of the equipment at the end of its useful life.

The higher the residual, the lower the lease payments will be during the term of the lease. The lease payments for different residuals for an asset costing $100000 at an interest rate of 10 per cent over a four-year term are shown in table 7.2.

Table 7.2: lease residuals

Lease residual	Monthly lease payment
20%	$2178
30%	$2009
40%	$1840
50%	$1671

Leasing companies have limits on residuals based on the type of equipment, the lease term, the equipment's intended use and your credit rating. Despite these limits, most leasing companies can be very generous because the more they can lower the payments, the more equipment they can convince borrowers to buy. Convincing you to borrow more is good for them in the short term, because they are under pressure to sell more equipment and the sales reps and lease brokers are paid commission on sales volumes. But it is bad for you because it artificially inflates your profits in the short term (and your income tax bill) and puts you at risk of getting into more debt later on.

Having a residual higher than the realistic salvage value at the end of the lease term puts you at risk of having to fund a shortfall because the price you get for the equipment at the end of the term leaves you short of the lease residual. Unless you have been putting away extra money to pay for this over the years it takes you by surprise and sends you into more debt when you need to lease replacement equipment.

86 When buying a business, do your research

Keep borrowing to a minimum when buying an existing business. The best way to do this is to make sure you aren't paying too much for it. The revenues and profits are almost always lower than you expect and the operating costs and expenses are almost always higher.

When you want to buy an existing business, get your accountant to check over the books and explain to you in detail exactly how the business makes money. Always look into several businesses for sale and investigate each one in detail.

By doing this you and your accountant will usually be able to put together a very good picture of how businesses in that industry work, including growth prospects, margins, cash flows, input costs, supplier terms, customer terms, stock turnover, effectiveness of different types of marketing, staffing requirements and IT needs.

You will often be asked to sign a confidentiality agreement before being allowed to see the books, but that's okay because you're not going to steal any trade secrets or customer lists. You're just getting an in-depth look at how the numbers work.

At the very least, this research will help you find the true value of the business and you will avoid paying too much for it, avoiding excessive debt. Often this type of research allows you to put together your own business plan and start your own business without having to buy one. I've lost count of the number of business owners who have said to me, 'Instead of buying this business I could have done it much better and cheaper myself if I'd done more research instead of rushing in'.

With most small businesses there are no real hard assets that can be transferred to the new owner. The main asset is often the personal relationships the current owner has with suppliers and customers. A new owner shouldn't pay much for this goodwill as they need to build their own personal relationships with suppliers and customers. Most suppliers insist on new terms with a new owner. Most retail leases require the approval of the landlord before the lease can be assigned, so the lease is not really an asset. Most retail centres have high turnover of tenants and there are always opportunities for choosing your own site.

Customers are fickle and they quickly notice a change of ownership. They are quick to stop buying if service or quality drops, but they are just as quick to tell others if you make improvements.

The bottom line is this: in most cases it is better and cheaper to start your own small business than to buy an existing one, as long as you do your homework. Never let yourself get rushed into buying a business. You can never do too much research.

87 Don't borrow to buy a franchise

There are more than 1000 different franchise systems in Australia. There are probably only a dozen or so I can think of that are worth paying money to buy into. For the rest, the franchise is probably not worth the money.

Most franchises are not really businesses with any real value, and thus cannot be sold after several years. In most cases the franchisees walk away when they have had enough, so it is really just a temporary income—and it's hard work in all the cases I have ever seen. So why pay good money to buy into it at the start? And why borrow?

Many franchise systems are designed primarily to make money for the franchisor. They 'churn and burn' new franchisees because there is a seemingly endless supply of new retirees and retrenched people willing to buy to join a system with their fresh wads of retirement or retrenchment money.

When doing your research on a franchise system, talk to lots of existing franchisees. You can talk to the ones suggested by the franchisor company but they will be 'yes men' and often they are paid kickbacks for helping sign up new franchisees. Always seek out and talk to several existing franchisees not on the franchisor's list. They are much more likely to give you the real story. The more franchisees you talk to the more you will learn—you can never talk to too many. Also talk to franchisees in competing systems to get their side of the story on the system you are considering and their system as well.

Most franchises are personal service jobs where you have to do all or most of the work, such as mowing lawns, washing dogs and cleaning houses or offices, yourself. If you really want to mow lawns, wash dogs and clean houses, put an ad in the local paper and work will come. You will keep all the profits yourself instead of paying a cut to the franchisor and you won't have to outlay any cash for goodwill or overpriced equipment or supplies. Consumers and businesses everywhere are always looking for good, reliable, honest people to do all kinds of things. Your ability to get work from referrals or repeat business will depend entirely on your own personal workmanship, quality, service and integrity, not whether you are part of some franchise. If you provide great service at a great price your business will grow. Pretty soon you will have to put on helpers to handle the volume. Charge them a fee for joining your system and before you know it you will be running your own franchise! Now that's a business that has real value and you can sell it for real money.

If, after all your research, you still want to buy a franchise, minimise borrowing. If it's your own money you can write it off if things go wrong, but if it's on debt you can't. The lender will hound you for years to get back the money, as well as interest and fees.

88 Be careful of line-of-credit mortgages for business

With a line-of-credit mortgage you pay a higher interest rate for the flexibility of being able to make irregular payments at irregular times, so make sure you get the best use out of it. They are most useful to fund a business or investment where the cash flow is irregular and the interest is tax deductible.

However, if you plan to fund the investment for a fixed period (for example, for buying an investment property or shares for a planned period of 10 years) where the cash flows are more or less regular (for example, from rent or dividend income) it is usually much better to use a separate no-frills loan, rather than a line of credit. The interest rate will be lower and it is easier to claim the interest as a tax deduction where there is a separate loan, rather than the loan being mixed up with borrowings for other purposes in the line of credit.

The flexibility of lines of credit can be very useful for funding business cash flows. But it is still usually better to structure the debt so that the core long-term debt is a long-term principal-and-interest loan, then take out a separate line of credit on top also secured by the same property (usually your main house). This way most of the debt is at a lower rate with regular principal and interest payments and you are paying the higher line-of-credit interest rate only on the smaller line-of-credit amount where you really need the flexibility.

Once you set up a separate line of credit for business, make sure you never use the cash drawn out of a line of credit for non-business purposes. The interest will not be tax deductible for the non-business portion. The Tax Office will start to view the whole arrangement as a mechanism to reduce tax and it may disallow tax deductions on any money drawn down from the account, even the money used for business purposes.

89 Use supplier terms and customer terms sensibly

Supplier terms and customer terms are the lifeblood of a business, but many small businesses don't use them to maximise cash flow and minimise debt. The aim is to not have to finance your inventory and operating expenses with debt; that is, to not have to outlay cash to pay for your inventory and operating expenses. For example, if your supplier terms are 60 days (that is, if you pay your suppliers an average of 60 days after delivery of the inventory) and if you hold inventory for an average of 40 days, then you can avoid financing your inventory with debt if you can get your customers to pay in less than 20 days from sale. If you can avoid financing your inventory and your expenses you can reduce your level of debt in the business substantially.

If your suppliers don't offer any discount or other benefits for paying up front, extend the payments for as long as possible before any late payment penalties cut in. Many suppliers start charging interest if payments are made later than a set period, such as 60 days after delivery or invoice.

If a supplier offers a discount for payment up front, work out whether it makes sense to use this or not. For example, if they offer a 5 per cent discount for paying up front instead of paying in, say, 90 days, this means their 90-day terms are effectively returning around 21.6 per cent per year, so it is worth using your overdraft at a rate of, say, 15 per cent interest to pay the supplier up front to get the supplier's discount.

On the other hand, if the discount is only 3 per cent for cash or 90-day terms, this annual rate is effectively lower than the overdraft rate, so it is not worth paying cash to get the discount.

'Customer terms' refer to the practice of allowing customers to pay for your goods and services after a period of time (such as 14 or 30 days), rather than getting payment when the sale is made. Many small businesses offer customer terms when there is no real need for it. Often when I buy goods or services from businesses I am perfectly happy to pay by cash, cheque or credit card up front, but they offer to invoice me via mail or email instead. Why give me 14 or 30 days to pay when I am happy to pay up front? Then there is the added cost of preparing and sending the invoice, the extra bookkeeping work and the risk of bad debts.

Sometimes, when I ask the business owner why they do this, they tell me it's how their 'system' does it, or what their competitors do, or that they would lose business if they charged up front.

This is bad logic for two reasons. The first is that customers generally buy on the basis of the quality, service and price, not on what terms you provide. If customers are choosing your business because of your customer terms, then you are not differentiating your business, and this is generally fatal for any business.

It is also bad logic because your competitors may be also offering terms because they see you doing it. If you insisted on customers paying up front, you may find that your competitors will soon follow you, so you will not have lost any competitive position.

Even if you do cut out customer terms, the customer gets an interest-free period anyway if they pay by credit card, so why give them a second interest-free period? By cutting down or cutting out customer terms you can dramatically improve your cash flow and reduce your borrowing needs in the business.

90 *Sell your debtors*

Many businesses go broke or have to take on extra debt because of slow-paying customers (debtors). Many specialist finance companies offer a service called factoring (also called debtor financing). The finance company buys your debtors and pays you cash, minus a discount, then collects the debts from your customers. This immediately frees up cash for your business.

It is a relatively expensive form of financing, but for many businesses it is not a case of comparing the relative cost of finance; it is a case of getting hold of cash or risk blowing the overdraft, or losing your supplier terms and even your relationship with suppliers. You may receive, say, only 80 per cent of the amount owing, but often this is better than receiving nothing at all, or receiving 100 per cent after a long battle involving lawyers.

Factoring your debtors can also mean you prevent what are short-term debts from becoming long-term, core debts, which are often hard to reduce. Many businesses collect no interest on outstanding debts owing to them, but pay interest on loans used to finance the debtors, so it makes sense to get cash in as quickly as possible then use it to pay off debt. One major advantage of debtor financing is that it can allow you to raise money quickly and often without having to put up security in the form of real estate or a charge over the business.

A similar form of financing is 'invoice discounting'. With invoice discounting you retain control of the collection of debts, whereas in factoring you're giving up control of the collection process to the factoring company. In many small businesses it's better to outsource the collection process to a professional factoring company, so you and your staff can get on with running the business.

91 Maximise depreciation

Capital items used in the business that have a useful life of more than one year can be deprecated over their useful life. For example, if you buy an item for $100 000, you cannot write off the whole $100 000 in the year that you bought it to get a tax deduction for the whole ammount in the first year. You can write off the $100 000 over a number of years and get a tax deduction in each year.

Of course, the total depreciation you can claim cannot be more than the capital cost of the item, so for a $100 000 machine the most you can claim in total depreciation is still $100 000. It is a question of timing when you get the tax benefit. The sooner you get the tax benefit, the sooner you can use the cash to pay off debt in the business.

There are two main ways to maximise your tax deductions for depreciation and use them to reduce debt. The first is to choose the best period in which to write off the cost. Under Australian tax law, you can nominate your own estimate of the effective life of most assets you depreciate. The shorter the effective life you nominate, the greater the depreciation expense and tax deduction each year. But the effective life nominated must be 'reasonable' or it will not be allowed by the Tax Office. For example, if you buy a machine for $100 000 that will last about 10 years, you cannot depreciate it over just two years by claiming a tax deduction of $50 000 each year for two years. But you might argue that the expected life in your business is seven or eight years, based on how you intend to use it and when you expect to upgrade the machine or trade it in for a new machine. The shorter the estimated life is, the sooner you get the tax benefits.

The second way to get tax benefits sooner is to maximise the depreciation rate. For most assets you can choose either the diminishing value method or the prime cost method. The diminishing value method will give you more tax benefits in the early years. For example, if you operate through a company paying the 30 per cent corporate tax rate and are depreciating a $100 000 asset over five years, the prime cost method gives you a tax benefit of $6000 per year for five years. The diminishing value method gives you a tax benefit of $9000 in year 1, $6300 in year 2, then lower amounts in the later years. Use this extra cash to pay off debt more quickly.

Assets costing less than $1000 can be depreciated immediately, resulting in a full tax deduction in the year it is purchased. Also, most assets costing more than $1000, and with effective lives of less than 25 years, can be pooled and depreciated at 30 per cent per year.

Talk to your accountant to make sure you are getting the maximum tax benefits of depreciation.

92 Never pay full price for business equipment

Business owners should never pay full retail price for business equipment. You can save many thousands of dollars buying smarter. Since most business equipment is bought using debt, you can keep the level of debt in your business much lower if you buy for less. Try these purchasing methods.

$ *Auction houses*. There are commercial auction houses in every major city where you can buy all sorts of items new, complete with packaging and warranty, for around 50 per cent of the retail price.

$ *Online*. A variety of commercial online sites offer a huge range of equipment at very low prices because they don't have high overheads.

$ *Discount outlets*. Even consumer retail outlets offer much lower prices for everyday items, especially consumables like stationery and office furniture.

$ *Wholesale outlets and distributors*. These are usually much cheaper and are set up to deal with business owners.

Often it is just a question of asking for a lower price because you are a business. You will be amazed how often this works.

Ask other businesses in your area (but not businesses that are competing with you) how they saved money on equipment.

Most new business owners have trouble estimating the level of volume and size of equipment needed in their business. Many end up with equipment far too big or small for their needs, which is inefficient and costly. The more research you do beforehand, including talking to other business owners about their experiences, the better.

93 Business succession to reduce debt

Three of the biggest problems faced by many small business owners are: how to get cash out of the business to reduce debt, how to retain good staff and how to sell out for a good price. There is a simple way of solving these problems.

As the business grows, its accounts may look very healthy and profitable. However, the owner can't get cash out to pay off debt because the value of the business is tied up in assets such as inventory, debtors and equipment. Often the only way to get your hands on the cash to pay out debt is to sell the business. For many small businesses, you can't really 'sell' the business because the business is not really a going concern without you, the owner and driver of the business, and with no guarantee that the other key staff will stay on either.

One possible solution is to help your key senior staff buy into the business. They can borrow money from a bank or you can finance them into it (make sure you take security over their house or other assets, just as a bank would). If the staff borrow from a bank you get the lump sum so you can pay off your business debt or mortgage. Alternatively, if you finance them into it, they pay you a regular payment instead because you are the 'bank'—and you can use these payments to reduce your debts progressively. This type of structured sale locks senior staff into the business and gives them a financial and emotional stake in it, which ensures they are committed to its continued success.

If you want to stay in the business for several years you can sell it to the staff in stages with the price for each stage based on a mutually agreed formula. That way senior staff can start by buying a small stake in the business for a modest amount in the initial stages, resulting in a higher total price for you as the business grows in value. Make sure you talk to your accountant and lawyer first about how to achieve the best outcome.

Part VIII

Avoiding and minimising debt

The most basic rules of building wealth are to spend less than you earn, and never borrow to pay for anything that depreciates in value. This includes cars, furniture, appliances and renovations. The most important practice to avoid is borrowing to pay for things that have no monetary value at all, such as living expenses or holidays.

You should only borrow to buy assets that appreciate in value at a higher rate than the interest rate on the loan, or that you use to generate business or investment income in excess of the interest paid. The only exceptions are:

$ a mortgage to buy your first home (or first home of your own after a divorce or separation). However, save enough to pay 10 to 20 per cent of the deposit and then pay the mortgage off as quickly as possible. For all subsequent houses pay cash. Don't forget that a mortgage is *not* 'good debt'; it is a necessary evil, so only borrow to get into the market and then pay it off as soon as possible.

$ a loan to buy your first car if you need it to get to work to start earning money. Save at least a 20 per cent deposit, then pay if off as quickly as possible. For all subsequent cars pay cash.

For all other things, if you can't pay cash you can't afford it. It's as simple as that—there's no getting around it.

The following sections discuss several things you can do to minimise the chances of getting into trouble with debt.

94 Maintain an emergency cash fund

Having an emergency fund goes a long way towards ensuring that you don't get into debt each time something unexpected happens that affects your finances. Many people seem to spend their entire lives lurching from one money crisis to the next, never getting out of debt and never being in control. Having an emergency fund can help prevent this happening.

Everybody should have an emergency cash fund ready for when it is needed in real emergencies; for example, when the fridge needs replacing, the car breaks down, or to cover living expenses if you suffer a temporary loss of income. How much you need in your emergency fund depends on your circumstances. A good guide is to have approximately three months of after-tax income. If you don't have protection in the form of income protection insurance, trauma insurance or comprehensive car insurance, you will need more in your emergency fund.

Keep your emergency cash fund separate from your main transaction account. If you keep savings in your transaction account they will soon disappear in everyday expenses. Open a separate high-interest-rate internet account and direct a small amount of money each pay day into the account. Once it has built to the desired level, you can either leave it in a high-rate account or transfer it to a bank term deposit and keep rolling it over at the end of each term. The advantage of term deposits is that they pay high rates of interest (often higher than the rates on cash accounts) and they are hard to access, but they can still be broken into in a genuine emergency. You may get a slightly lower interest rate if you break a term deposit early, but this will happen only rarely.

And remember: a shoe sale is not an emergency!

95

Use separate accounts for savings goals

Once you have an emergency cash fund set up and growing, set up a separate high-interest-rate savings account for each specific savings goal you may have, such as a house deposit, new car, holiday, boat or Christmas presents. Each account should be separate and named after the purpose of the account; for example, you might call your house deposit account 'the Jones house deposit account'. This helps you resist the temptation to raid the account to pay for everyday items and it motivates you to put more money into it whenever you can.

Having separate savings accounts for specific goals means you have the cash ready when you need it and you don't need to go into debt to buy the items. Setting up the accounts also helps you think about what is really important to you and worth making the effort to save for.

You can make contributions to the savings accounts from your pay—most employers are happy to split salaries into separate accounts. That way the money doesn't sit in your transaction account where it can be spent.

Restrict access to these accounts. Most high-interest-rate internet accounts come with a host of access options such as ATM access, internet access, EFTPOS and card access. The best way to save is to cut off all possible means of access; simply don't set up any of these access options when you open the account. Even set up a separate internet login ID so you aren't tempted to make internet transfers between accounts. If you have several separate savings accounts set up you can link these to one internet login ID so you can see the balances of the savings accounts on the one screen, but make it a different login ID to your other bank accounts (such as your main transaction account, home loan and cards). That way you will never be tempted to break into the savings accounts and use them for everyday expenses.

96 No deposit, no mortgage

A mortgage is a huge commitment that binds you to a contract to make payments every month for the term of the loan, which can be up to 30 years of your life. You are agreeing to make payments each month for decades to come, whether your income goes up or down, whether you have a job or not, and regardless of whatever else happens in the economy or in your personal life.

If you haven't been able to save a deposit for a house, it's a sure sign that you're not ready for this type of commitment yet. If you haven't been able to put money away every month for a few years to build a deposit, what makes you think you will suddenly start doing it every month for the next 25 or 30 years? With a mortgage there is no room for excuses—if you miss your repayments they take your house.

Apart from providing proof to yourself and lenders that you have the discipline to make regular payments, having a deposit also gives you a buffer to protect you when property values fall. If you get into financial trouble and have to sell, without an equity buffer you can end up owing more than the house is worth. Even after they take your house, the lender can still come after you for any shortfall. You can lose all your other assets, and the bad credit rating you get can prevent you starting over for years.

If you have less than a 20 per cent deposit you pay a higher interest rate and have to pay expensive mortgage insurance, which keeps you in debt for years longer than necessary.

Governments often offer handouts like grants to first home buyers to get them into the market. Despite the way they are marketed, these handouts are not a deposit for the buyer, they're really just subsidies for property developers. These political handouts are generally higher for new houses than for existing houses because property developers (who pocket grants for new houses) are a major source of political party funding.

You should never count these grants and handouts as part of your deposit. You never actually get your hands on the cash, it goes straight from the government to the vendor on settlement. If you buy a house for $300 000 and use $21 000 in grants, and another, say, $20,000 in developer subsidies or so-called 'incentives', the real purchase price is only $259 000 and the true value is even less, because with new houses on remote estates most of the price goes towards improvements and fitout which depreciate rapidly.

By all means take advantage of any taxpayer-funded handouts and property developer subsidies on offer, but remember that these are not deposits. Make sure you also have a healthy deposit saved.

Using a credit card or personal loan as a deposit is also a big mistake for the same reason, because it's not your money, you didn't have to save for it and it doesn't give you an equity buffer because it's just another debt. Taking on a huge financial commitment without having practised and established the discipline and good financial habits is a sure road to financial ruin.

Until the 1980s, banks required a 20 per cent cash deposit to buy a house, plus several years of proven savings history with the bank. In the mortgage 'innovation' of the lending boom of the late 1990s and 2000s, all lenders loosened their lending rules, even the boring old big banks. Loans for 90 per cent of the purchase price became commonplace and pretty soon some lenders were offering 95 per cent loans, then 100 per cent loans and even 103 and 106 per cent loans to pay for the costs associated with buying a house. 'Buy a house with no money down'—what a great innovation!

Don't fall into the trap of going into a mortgage without proving to yourself that you have the discipline and financial habits necessary to take on the commitment. Save hard for a deposit and, in the meantime, do plenty of research into where to buy for the best long-term capital growth. Remember that a house is not an investment, it's a savings plan. Only very well located residential property (property close to transport, employment, shops, cafes, schools, medical services, parks, beaches and so on) increases in value over the long term by more than mortgage interest rates, so you get ahead only if you do your research and buy well, then pay it off quickly. Rather than rushing in to buy a new 'dream home' in the outer suburbs with little or no deposit, spend a couple of years saving hard for a real deposit and spend the time researching the market in areas offering more potential capital growth.

97 Renters, get a 10 to 15 per cent discount on your first home

Here's a way of turning dead rent money into a home of your own, keeping the purchase price low and minimising the size of your mortgage. I've seen this work many times successfully.

If you like the place you have been renting and want to stay in the same area, ask the owner if you can take over the mortgage and buy the house from them. Do your homework to find out the home's real value and then offer them, say, 10 to 15 per cent less than the value of the home. The owner might want to sell and be happy to sell quickly to someone they know and trust, rather than face the uncertainty and time delays of trying to sell it on the open market. Plus they save on selling costs such as agent's commission and advertising, which can be up to 5 per cent of the price, and they don't miss out on rent if you were to vacate while they try to sell. For an owner, getting 10 per cent less than the market value on a simple, quick, clean sale with no selling costs and no vacancy period can be an attractive option.

This approach results in you obtaining an instant credit rating, a discount on the purchase price, lower upfront loan fees and a smaller mortgage than you would otherwise have. You've turned dead rent money into a home of your own and you don't even have to move!

The owner can give you a credit reference if you have been making regular rent payments with no arrears. Go to the owner's existing lender and they will already have the security documentation on file (title deeds, valuation and so on) so you save money on upfront fees. You won't actually take over the owner's mortgage. It is a new loan in your name, but you're making it easy for the lender to approve it.

When buying from your landlord, always make sure you actually buy the house by signing a transfer and that you borrow from a recognised bank, building society or credit union. Don't be lured into a vendor finance agreement where you only receive the title after the last payment. There are lots of shady vendor finance schemes around that should be avoided at all costs. In all cases get proper advice from a lawyer you choose yourself, not one recommended by the landlord or mortgage broker.

You can also use this plan to buy your parents' or grandparents' house if you are looking to buy your first house and they are looking to downsize.

It may not be your perfect dream home, but nothing ever is. It is generally much better to buy an established house (even if it's run-down) in an established inner suburb that is near transport, employment, shops and services, than a new house in a remote new housing estate miles from anywhere.

98 Don't borrow to put money into superannuation

In Australia, the superannuation system has many benefits. The main benefits are that employer contributions are compulsory and the money is locked up and can't be accessed until you reach a certain age. There are also several tax benefits, but in most cases these are more than eaten up by fees and sales commissions ripped out of your superannuation fund investments.

Be very wary of schemes promoted by some financial planners to get you to borrow money to invest in superannuation. While mathematically there may be some benefit in some very limited circumstances for some people, there are several problems with many of these schemes, including the following:

$ the planner usually takes a sales commission from the lending side, as well as an ongoing trailing commission out of each monthly loan payment

$ the planner also takes a sales commission out of the superannuation investment, as well as another ongoing trailing commission on the investment inside your superannuation account

$ the planner also charges ongoing fees (such as platform fees, wrap fees and administrative fees) every year on the additional amount in your superannuation fund

$ all of these fees and commissions come out of your pocket and reduce your investment returns

$ the interest you pay on the loan is not tax deductible because it generates no assessable income to you

$ in most cases the contributions to the super fund are 'undeducted' or 'non-concessional' (made out of after-tax money), so you get no tax deduction for the contributions.

The only situation in which the tax benefits of superannuation outweigh the cost of commissions and fees is where you are in a high tax bracket, make tax-deductible contributions, manage your own fund and invest the money directly yourself where you minimise fees and costs. Always obtain detailed advice from your regular accountant before entering into any such scheme.

99 Avoid tax-based schemes

The golden rule regarding the borrowing of money to bring about a tax benefit is: never buy anything primarily for tax reasons. Every investment must make sense on its own merits. Any tax advantage you gain is merely an added bonus.

In the couple of weeks leading up to the end of each financial year in Australia (30 June) thousands of people borrow more than $1 billion each year to put into all sorts of schemes and scams dreamt up by investment bankers and other schemers and scammers. Many of these schemes are outright frauds and investors never get their money back. Even in those that are legitimate, most of the money is usually skimmed off by the promoters, the management companies, the lenders, lawyers and other hangers-on.

In Australia, tax-based schemes usually involve financing exotic animals, birds or crops. Others are complex capital-guaranteed or capital-protected schemes to buy shares or managed funds, but they are riddled with layers and layers of fees and commissions ripped out by the investment banks. The best rule is never to go near anything marketed heavily around the end of June that promises to save a fortune in tax. (In fact, a good rule in general is to never touch anything conjured up by investment bankers!)

If you are already in one of these schemes, make it your mission to find out exactly where your money has gone, who has it and what they are doing with it. Unfortunately in most of these schemes you are locked in for several years and there is no secondary market so you can't sell. If you are supposed to have received some kind of ownership rights in a plantation, vineyard or a flock of ostriches, take a trip and find out with your own eyes if it actually exists and, if so, exactly which part is yours. Hassle and hound everybody associated with the scheme until you get the answers you are looking for.

A good place to start is <www.fido.gov.au>. Look in the scams and warnings section.

100 Be careful if guaranteeing other people's debts

This is a very sensitive area because it usually involves family, which can often lead to disputes that become personal. Generally, if you are sharing the benefits and control of an asset, then it is fine to borrow jointly or guarantee to someone else's debt; for example, spouses or partners buying a house to live in together, or a business they jointly control and operate.

Problems arise when one party guarantees business debts of the partner or family member where the guarantor (the person providing the guarantee to the lender) has no input or control in the business. Examples include people guaranteeing the business debts of adult children or grandchildren.

Often first-time business owners need a guarantor to guarantee their bank loan while they build their own credit rating. New business ventures are always extremely risky and the probability of guarantors losing their money is very high. Always put a dollar limit on your guarantee and make sure it is set out in the guarantee document you sign. If the borrower is borrowing $100 000, limit your guarantee to $100 000 so you are not liable for any more if the borrower runs up huge debts. Always put a time limit on the guarantee, such as two or three years, and make sure it is in the mortgage document.

Never, ever, ever sign a guarantee without obtaining your own legal advice from your own lawyer. Never use the same lawyer used or recommended by the borrower, lender or mortgage broker. A few hundred dollars spent on a lawyer now could save you many hundreds of thousands of dollars later.

If you have guaranteed somebody else's debt, now might be a good time to review the relationship. In the time since they took out the loan, they should have built up their own credit rating and credit history, so the lender should be happy for you to remove the guarantee and let the borrower stand on their own two feet.

If the lender is willing to drop your guarantee but will charge the borrower a higher interest rate on their loan, you need to make the borrower aware of the value of your guarantee. If you do continue with the guarantee you should charge the borrower the difference in interest rates as a guarantee fee. The lender's higher interest means the lender is adding an extra margin for the extra risk of the borrower. You are carrying this risk so you need to be compensated for it by charging the borrower.

If the lender won't let you drop the guarantee because the borrower has a poor payment history during the period of the guarantee, this should ring alarm bells. You are running a real risk of the borrower defaulting and being called on to cough up the money to pay out the debt. If you don't have the spare cash ready to pay, it is time to have the borrower make their own arrangements to pay out the debt.

101 Beware the lender who *says* you can afford a loan

I have lived and worked through four great financial booms and the collapses that followed them: the lending boom of the early 1980s that resulted in the 1982–83 recession, the 'greed is good' boom of the late 1980s that resulted in the 1987 crash and the 1990–91 recession, the late 1990s dotcom boom that resulted in the 2000–01 tech-wreck (which Australia avoided because we don't have a large technology sector), and the late 1990s/early 2000s boom which resulted in the 2008–09 credit crisis.

The patterns for each lending boom and bust cycle are very similar. In the booms, lenders lend like drunken sailors and all this new money from debt pushes asset prices way beyond their true values. Lenders come up with all sorts of lending innovations that are mostly just new ways to get more people to buy things they can't afford.

Booms always collapse into busts. When people (and businesses) start falling behind on payments they could never afford in the first place, banks panic and suddenly go from recklessly lending to anyone who asks for a loan to not lending to anyone at all, which strangles businesses, forcing them to lay off workers. Incomes fall, asset prices fall, unemployment rises, thousands of businesses fail and hundreds of thousands of people lose their jobs, assets and homes, and are destroyed financially.

Most borrowers borrow only a few times in their lives, but the lenders, mortgage brokers and finance brokers handle loans every day of the week. They are the so-called experts. So when a lender or broker says 'You can afford it', you naturally believe them. Big mistake!

Finance brokers and mortgage brokers don't have any incentive to worry about whether you can make the repayments for the next 30 years. They're not taking the credit risk. They get most of their sales commission up front, then move on to the next deal. By the time the collapse comes they're long gone. Bankers and other lenders don't care either. Their salaries and bonuses are based mainly on new loan volumes and current revenues, and they don't carry the credit risk. They've sold the high-risk part to some insurance company via mortgage insurance, which you pay for, not the lender, and they've sold your loan to bondholders somewhere on the other side of the world. The car salespeople or furniture retailers don't care either. They get paid for selling cars and furniture and upfront commissions from the finance they stitch you up with.

The only person who knows and really cares if you can afford the loan is you. You are responsible for your own finances. No, you can't buy a house with a couple of hundred dollars on your credit card! There's no such thing as even one month 'interest free', let alone three years interest free! You can't have the keys to a new car with no money down and zero per cent interest! If it sounds too good to be true, it probably is—and it will probably get you into a whole lot of financial strife you will regret for many years to come.

Sure, mortgage brokers, finance brokers and bankers are not all sharks. But how can you tell the difference? And why take the risk? Take your time, don't get rushed into anything, ask friends and family, do your own numbers, shop around, do plenty of research into what you are buying, and make your own decision on what you can afford. Keep things simple and avoid complex schemes. Ask plenty of questions. If you don't understand something it usually means that they don't want you to understand it. Keep asking questions until you do.

This is the only way to control your debts, otherwise they will end up controlling you.

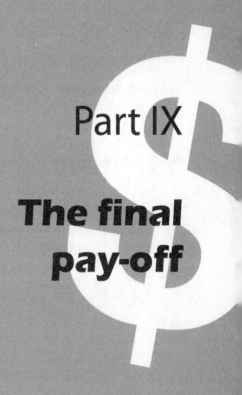

Part IX

The final pay-off

If you want to get out of debt and stay out of debt there are a host of ideas in this book that just about anybody can use, starting today—literally—from your home or work. With the power of mobile phones and the internet there are several steps you can take right now without even getting out of your chair! The key is to start small and start today.

I sometimes have frustrating conversations with readers who are motivated at the start, but get bogged down in decisions such as whether to pay an extra $100 per month off the mortgage, or whether to make it $200 instead, or whether to attack the credit card or the personal loan first. The problem is that months later when I ask them how they are going they still haven't started! Other priorities come along in their busy lives and somehow it just falls between the cracks and nothing gets done.

It is much better to start small initially. If you start in a big way, it may be too much of an adjustment and you may give up and never re-start the plan. If you start out small, you can always accelerate the plan once you see how easy it is. When you start seeing real progress you will want to increase your efforts and before long you are well on the way to getting out of debt and on the path to financial freedom.

Start small and start today—you will stick to the plan and you will win the war on debt!

Part X

Useful resources

There are several websites where you can compare products, interest rates, fees, and so on. They also contain many useful and interesting articles:

$ <www.yourmortgage.com.au>

$ <www.infochoice.com.au>

$ <www.cannstar.com.au>

$ <www.ratecity.com.au>

$ <www.choice.com.au>.

You can also use bank and other lender websites, but be warned that they are designed to encourage you to borrow more, not less!

The following organisations provide free financial counselling.

Australian Capital Territory	Care Inc. Financial Counselling Service 02 6257 1788
New South Wales	Financial Counsellors Association of NSW 0500 888 079 <www.financialcounsellors.asn.au> CreditLine Helpline 1800 808 488
Northern Territory	Anglicare Northern Territory Financial Counselling Service 08 8985 0000 Somerville Community Services (Darwin area) 08 8920 4100 Tangentyre Council (Alice Springs area) 08 8953 7649
Queensland	Financial Counselling Queensland Network 07 3321 3192 <www.fcqn.asn.au>
South Australia	South Australian Financial Counsellors Association <www.safca.info > UnitingCare Wesley 08 8202 5111 Department for Families and Communities 08 8304 0120
Tasmania	Anglicare Financial Counselling Service 1800 243 232 Consumer Credit Solicitor at Hobart Community Legal Service 03 6223 2500 or 1800 232 500
Victoria	Consumer Affairs Victoria 1300 558 181

Western Australia	Financial Counsellors Resource Project 08 9221 9411 Consumer Credit Legal Service 08 9221 7066 Financial Counsellors' Association of WA 08 9325 1617

Also try these:

$ Financial Information Service (FIS). Free call 13 2300; <www.centrelink.gov.au>

$ Centrelink Personal/Family Counselling Service. Free call 131 794

$ CRS Australia. Free call 1800 277 277; <www.crsaustralia.gov.au>

$ Lifeline. Free call 13 11 14

$ <www.understandingmoney.gov.au.>.

Top 10 ways to control and minimise debt

1 Spend less than you earn—never spend money you don't have.

2 Never borrow to pay living expenses or to buy items that decrease in value.

3 Never re-draw money you've already paid off a loan—paying it off once is hard enough.

4 Only use a credit card if you know you can pay the full balance each month—never carry a balance into next month.

5 Make your own decisions on what you can afford—never trust a lender, mortgage broker or credit card company who says 'you can afford it'.

6 Don't get rushed into anything—take your time and ask lots of questions until you get answers that make sense.

7 Avoid complex schemes—the simplest solutions are usually the best.

8 Almost all optional extras on loans are a waste of money, and/or are designed to get you into more debt and to keep you in debt for longer—keep it simple and opt for the lowest overall cost, then concentrate on paying it off quickly.

9 There's no such thing as 'interest-free' periods, 'low introductory rates', or buying anything for 'no money down'—you always end up paying for it in the end—the less cash you put into it now, the more it ends up costing in the long run.

10 Always leave a margin of safety for when things go wrong—because they usually do: house prices do fall, interest rates do rise, incomes do fall, employers and businesses do fail.

Top five ways to win the war on debt

1 Make a plan, set targets and take action—don't just drift along.

2 Always pay more than the minimum repayment on loans—even tiny additional amounts can save a fortune in interest and get you out of debt much sooner.

3 Use part of your pay-rises and tax cuts to increase your repayments each year.

4 Attack one debt at a time—it's easier to focus your efforts—and early wins will motivate you to step up your efforts.

5 It's better to start small than not start at all—the sooner you start, the sooner you will be debt-free.

Index

accountants 161–162, 170–172, 182

accounts 114–115, 118–119, 176–178
—deposit 62–63, 176–177
—offset 62–64, 177–178
—savings 176–177

achievements, rewards for 135–136

advances, cash 107–110, 113–114, 132

American Express cards 117–121

Asian economic crisis 147

assets 5–6, 21
—business 61–62, 157–162, 170–171
—capital 158–159, 168–169
—depreciating 7, 22–24, 61, 65, 124, 127–128, 168–169, 173–174
—growth 90–91
—investment 62, 89–91, 137–138, 141, 147–148, 153–154, 173–174
—life of 160
—non-business 124–127
—security 133–134
—subprime loans and 71–72
—superannuation as 124

Australian Bureau of Statistics 153–157

Australian dollar 147–149

Australian economic boom 1–3

Australian property markets 146–147

Australian workers 63–64

bad debt 21–24, 70, 167

bankruptcy 26–27, 109

bank accounts 114–115, 118–119, 176–178

bank cheques 66

banks 19–20, 64–66, 82–85, 93, 102, 178

boat loans 6, 13, 24–25, 61, 92, 123–124, 133
bonds 143–144
—deposit 143–144
—government 91
booms, economic 1–2, 59–60, 146
borrowing *see* loans
brokers, mortgage 7, 50, 72–73, 79–80, 82–84, 93, 184–187, 194
budgets 47–48
business 153–154
—assets 61–62, 157–162, 170–171
—buying a new 161–162
—customer terms and 165–166
—debtors 167–168
—debts 21–22, 25, 153–154 165–169, 184
—equipment 157–159, 170–171
—equity 157–159
—franchises 163–164
—lines of credit and 76, 164–165
—operating costs 161
—personal finances and 155–156
—plan 156–157
—staff 171–172
—succession 171–172
—suppliers 156, 162, 165–166
—supplier terms and 165–166
—taxation and 89, 127

capital
—assets 158–159, 168–169
—growth 90–91
—purchases 157–158
—returns 143
capital gains tax 86, 139–140, 151
capitalising loans 65, 68–70
cars
—insurance for 107, 130–131
—loans for 6, 13, 18, 65, 73, 123–124, 126–127
—new 129–130
—paying off 25
—used 124, 128–129
cash 61, 91, 110, 118, 121, 132
—advances 107–110, 113–114, 132
—deposits 123–124, 126–128, 132, 143–144, 146
—depreciating items and 7–8, 22–24, 61, 65, 124, 127–128, 168–169, 173–174
—emergency fund 175–176
cash rate 50–51
charge cards 117–119
cheques, bank 66
consolidating debt 72–75, 109
credit
—charges 131
—limits 117–121
—lines of 64–66, 76, 119, 141–142, 164–165
—ratings 9–10, 26–27, 71, 104, 160, 177, 180
—reports 134–135
credit bureau 134–135

credit cards 2, 7–8, 13, 73,
105–106
—cash advances on 107–110,
113–114, 132
—choosing 108–111
—direct debits 114–115
—getting rid of 106, 116–117
—limits 75, 117–121, 134–
135
—paying off 25, 54–55,
116–117
—repayments on 111–116
—spending on 107–108
—statements 115
—store cards 131–132
—surfing 108–109
currency 146–148
customer terms 165–166

debt 1–9, 13–15, 22
—bad 21–24, 70, 167
—business 21–22, 25, 153–
154, 166–167, 184
—collectors 132
—consolidating 72–75, 109
—guaranteeing 183–184
—household 1–9, 22–23
—income versus 14–17
—minimising 173–187
—prioritising 24–28, 135
—succession of business to
reduce 171–172
debtors 167–168, 171
debt services ratio 17–18
debt-to-income ratio 14–17
deductions, tax 127–128,
143–145, 153–156, 169–170
deposit 126, 177–178
—accounts 62–63, 176–177
—bonds 143–145

—cash 123–124, 126–128,
132, 143–144, 146
—mortgages 177–178
—term 144, 175
depreciating assets 7–8, 22–24,
61, 65, 124, 127–128, 168–
169, 173–174
depreciation
—allowances 143
—maximising 168–170
direct debit 94, 114–115, 118,
125
disposable income 3–4
dividends 142, 151–152
dollar, Australian 147–147
downsizing mortgages 96–98
downturn, economic 6, 45, 146
dual incomes 80–82

economic crisis 3–4
economic cycles 50, 58-59, 100,
140–141, 151
economy 1–5
—boom 1–3, 59–60, 146
—surplus 3
education 21–22
emergency cash fund 175–176
equipment, business 157–159,
170–171
equity 150, 159
—business 157–159
—home 24, 56, 74, 144, 150
—negative 127–128
exchange rates 146–148

fees 16–18, 75–80, 20–21
—ad-hoc 20
—administrative 181
—annual 20, 76–78, 80, 108
—application 20, 53, 77
—back-end 20

fees (cont'd)
—front-end 20
—late-payment 16, 20
—legal 53, 79
—negotiating 79–80
—payout 17, 20, 78, 80
—processing 20, 77
—service 16–17
—settlement 20, 77
—statement 16, 18, 20
—transaction 16, 20
—upfront 54, 77
first home, buying 179–180
fixed-rate loans 58–60, 68–69, 140–141
floating-rate loans 58–60
franchises 163–164
franking rules 150, 151

government 1–3, 178–179
— bonds 91
growth, capital 90–91
guaranteeing debts 183–185
guarantors 18, 183–185

hobby farms 145–146
holiday houses 145–146
honeymoon rates 66–68, 70
household debt 1–9, 15–16, 22–23
houses see property
house-sitting 86–87

income 14–15
—currency 146–148
—disposable 3–4
—dual 80–82
—interest 119
—patterns 45–46
—rental 87

insurance 130–131, 143–144, 175
—car 107, 130–131
—mortgage 177, 186
—personal 130–131
—third-party 131
interest 5–6, 17, 19–22, 26, 31–40, 42–50, 84
—business debt 156, 165–166, 168–169
—cash advances and 107–110, 113–114, 132
—credit rating and 26–27
—fixed 58
—floating 58
—honeymoon rates 66–68
—investment bankers and 182–183
—loan-to-margin 149–150
—mortgages and 31–33, 36–40, 51–59, 61–62
—penalty 132
—personal debt and 156
—shopping for lower rates 66–68
—store loans and 131–132
—subprime loans and 71-73
—tax-deductable 22–23, 61–62, 86–87, 90
interest-free periods 14, 25, 108–109
interest-only loans 56–59
interest-rate changes 84–85
investment 1–6, 21–22, 89–93
—assets 62, 89–91, 137–138, 141, 147–148, 153–154, 173–174
—bankers 182–183
—loans 137–151

—long-term 141–142
—overseas 141–142
—properties 98, 139–141
—superannuation and 89–93

landlords 162–163, 180–182
late mortgage repayments 16, 20,
    132–133
law, taxation 169
lease term 158–159
lenders 5, 185–186
length of loans 43–44
line-of-credit mortgages 64–66,
    141–142, 164–165
lines of credit 64–66, 76, 119,
    141–142, 164–165
—for property 139–142
loans 18–19
—boat 6, 13, 24–25, 61, 92,
    123–124, 133
—capitalising 68–70
—car 6, 13, 18, 65, 73,
    123–124, 126–127
—fixed-rate 58–59, 68–69,
    140
—floating-rate 58–59
—guaranteeing 184–185
—honeymoon rates 66–68, 70
—investment 137–151
—late payment of 16, 20,
    132–133
—length of 43–44
—margin 14, 149–150
—penalties for early payment
    of 18, 53
—personal 123–124
—principal-and-interest
    56–57, 139–140
—priotitising 25
—renegotiating 125–156

—repayments 31, 34–35, 37,
    41–43, 47, 51–52
—security 18
—shares and 148–150
—special features 75
—store 110–111, 131–132
—subprime 71–72
—switching 53–54
—term 158–159
—variable-rate 104–141
loan term 158–159
loan-to-margin interest 149–150
loan-to-value ratio 149
long-term investments 90,
    141–142, 150, 158–159

margin loans 14, 149–150
minimising debt 173–187
mortgages 29–30, 174
—brokers and 7, 50, 72–73,
    79–80, 82–84, 93, 184–187,
    194
—capitalising loans 68–70
—consolidating debt and
    72–75
—deposit 177–178
—downsizing 96–98
—extra payments on 31–33
—fees 79–80
—final payment of 88–89,
    101–102
—first home 179–181
—fixed-interest 58–59, 68–69,
    140
—floating-interest 58–59
—honeymoon rates 66–68
—insurance 177, 186
—interest rates 31–33
—investing versus paying off
    89–90
—length of 43–45

mortgages *(cont'd)*
—line-of-credit 64–66, 141–142, 164–165
—margin loans 149–150
—offset accounts and 62–64, 177–178
—principal-and-interest 56, 139–140
—prioritising 25
—redraw 60–61
—repayments 31, 34–35, 37, 41–43, 47, 51–52
—schemes 102–103
—special features of 75
—subprime 71–72
—superannuation and 93–94, 98–99
—switching loans 53–54
—tax consequences of 23
—tenants and 85–87, 94–95, 162
—variable-rate 104–141

negative equity 127–128
non-business assets 124–127

offset accounts 62–64, 177–178
overdraft 157–158
overseas investments 141–142, 146–147

patterns, income 45–46
paying off credit card 25, 54–55, 116–117
payout two-step 101–102
penalties for early payment of loans 18, 53
penalty interest 132
personal debt 123–124, 156
personal finances 155–156

personal insurance 130–131
personal loans 123–124
principal-and-interest mortgages 56–57, 139–140
prioritising debts 24–28, 135
property 24, 56, 74, 96–100, 144, 150–151
—downsizing 96–97
—first home 179–180
—fixed-rate loans 140
—hobby farms 145–146
—holiday houses 145–146
—investment 98, 139–141
—lines of credit for 139–142
—market 98–99
—overseas investment in 146–147
—principle-and-interest loans and 125–126
—renovations 24, 100
—rental 85–86
—residential 140–141
—selling 103–104
purchases, capital 157–158

real estate 24, 56, 74, 96–100, 144, 150 *see also* property
redraw mortgages 60–61
refinancing 55, 125–126
refunds, tax 142–143, 151–152
renegotiating loans 125–126
rental properties 85–87, 140–141
repayments 28, 113–116, 141
—credit card 111–116
—mortgage 31, 34–35, 37, 41–43, 47, 51–52
—schedules 28
repossession 24–24, 104, 123–127, 132–133,
Reserve Bank of Australia 50
retirement 139–140

savings 1–3
—account 176–177
—changing attitudes towards
1–7
savings-to-debt ratio 2
security assets 133–134
security loans 18
share loans 148–149
shares 90–93, 142–143
—borrowing to buy 148–150
—buy-backs 143
small businesses 8, *see also* business
—debt 153–154
—finances 156
—staff 171
—starting 155–156
—tax and 153
staff 171–172
statements
—bank 115
—credit card 115
store cards 110–111, 131–132
subprime mortgages 71–72
succession, business 171–172
superannuation 5–6, 181–182
—assets 124

—investment and 89–93
—mortgages and 93–94,
98–99
—taxation and 182
suppliers 156, 162, 165–166

tax
—business and 89, 127 153
—cuts 42
—deductable interest 22–23,
61–62, 86–87, 90
—deductions 127–128,
143–145, 153–156, 169–170
—law 169
—refunds 142–143, 151–152
—superannuation and 182
tax-based schemes 182–183
tenants 85–87, 162
—children as 94–95
term deposits 144, 175
third-party insurance 131

unemployment 146–147

variable-rate loans 104–141
Veda Advantage Ltd 135